CULTURE SMART!
SLOVENIA

Jason Blake

·K·U·P·E·R·A·R·D·

ISBN 978 1 85733 600 9
This book is also available as an e-book: eISBN 978 1 85733 601 6

British Library Cataloguing in Publication Data
A CIP catalogue entry for this book is available from the British Library

First published in Great Britain 2011
by Kuperard, an imprint of Bravo Ltd
59 Hutton Grove, London N12 8DS
Tel: +44 (0) 20 8446 2440 Fax: +44 (0) 20 8446 2441
www.culturesmart.co.uk
Inquiries: sales@kuperard.co.uk

Distributed in the United States and Canada
by Random House Distribution Services
1745 Broadway, New York, NY 10019
Tel: +1 (212) 572-2844 Fax: +1 (212) 572-4961
Inquiries: csorders@randomhouse.com

Series Editor Geoffrey Chesler
Design Bobby Birchall

Printed in Malaysia

Cover image: *The façade of the People's Loan Bank building. Wiener Sezession architecture in Miklošičeva Cesta, Ljubljana.* © I.Middleton / Travel-Images.com

The photographs on pages 14 (bottom), 107, 108, and 133 are reproduced by permission of the author.

Images on the following pages reproduced under Creative Commons Attribution-Share Alike 3.0 Unported license: 13 © I, Michael Gäbler; 14 (top) © Annebethmi from English Wikipedia; 17 © David Edgar; 27 © xJaM; 64 © Ioscius; 66, 115, and 164 © Andrejj; 69 and 139 © Rude; 71 © MORS (Bruno Toič); 79 © Feri; 86 © zyance; 98 © Petar Milošević; 111 © Cecil; 120 © Orlovic; 124 © Ex13; 126 © Vijverln; 136 © LucasSi (talk); and 149 © I.

Images reproduced under Creative Commons Attribution-Share Alike 2.0 Generic license: 70 © Tony Bowden; 91 © discosour; 105 © 29cm; 106 © Jon Wick; 109 © juanma from Barcelona, Spain; and 119 © Lars Ploughmann. Under Creative Commons Attribution-Share Alike 2.5 Generic license: 43 © User Sweden @ sl.

Photo on page 93 © iStockphoto. The image on page 34 is photograph No. NA 15129 from the Imperial War Museum collection No. 4700-39.

About the Author

JASON BLAKE teaches in the English Department at the University of Ljubljana. Born and raised in Toronto, he has been living in Slovenia since 2000. In addition to a PhD in English literature, he has an MA in German, and before moving to Slovenia he spent over three years studying and working in Germany and Austria.

He has translated widely from Slovenian (as well as from German), primarily in the area of cultural studies. Among his published translations are five books, myriad articles, and more than a dozen short stories. He is the author of *Canadian Hockey Literature* and a book-length essay-writing guide that focuses on cultural differences between Slovenian and English writing. In 2007–8 he worked as a language trainer preparing civil servants for Slovenia's presidency of the European Union.

contents

Map of Slovenia 7
Introduction 8
Key Facts 10

Chapter 1: LAND AND PEOPLE 12
• Geography 12
• Climate 16
• The People 18
• A Brief History 20
• Government 38
• Politics 40
• Economic Transformation 42

Chapter 2: VALUES AND ATTITUDES 44
• Small and Western 44
• Identity—Defined by Language 45
• Religion 46
• After Communism 49
• Bureaucracy and Attitudes Toward Authority 50
• Self-Image 51
• What Do You Think of Us? 52
• Attitude Toward Western Foreigners 53
• Tolerance 53
• The Slovenian Sin: Sticking Out 55
• Attitudes Toward Education 56
• Status 57
• Work Ethic 59

Chapter 3: CUSTOMS AND TRADITIONS 60
• Holidays and Celebrations 60
• Christmas 60
• Carnival (Pust) 63
• Easter 64
• New Year 66
• All Saints' Day 67
• Other Occasions 68

• National Holidays 70
• Hatched, Matched, and Dispatched 74

Chapter 4: MAKING FRIENDS **78**
• Friends for Life 79
• Meeting People 80
• Conversation 81
• Humor 83
• Taboo Topics 84
• Invitations 86
• Manners 88
• Dating 89

Chapter 5: THE SLOVENIANS AT HOME **92**
• Family Life 92
• Schooldays 93
• After High School 96
• House and Home 97
• The Daily Round 100
• Shopping 101
• Employment 102

Chapter 6: TIME OUT **104**
• Vacations 104
• Sports 105
• Cultural Activities 109
• Cuisine 112
• Eating Out 114
• Banks and Paying 116

Chapter 7: TRAVEL, HEALTH, AND SAFETY **118**
• Getting to Slovenia 119
• Public Transportation 120
• Taxis 125
• Driving 126
• Cycling 129

contents

• Off the Beaten Path	129
• Where to Stay	130
• Key Destinations and Activities	132
• Health	134
• Safety	135
Chapter 8: BUSINESS BRIEFING	**136**
• Business Culture	137
• The Customer is Not Always the Boss	139
• Women in Business	141
• Meetings	141
• Presentations	143
• Negotiations	143
• Contracts	144
• Managing Disputes	145
Chapter 9: COMMUNICATING	**148**
• Language	148
• Body Language	154
• The Media	156
• Internet and E-mail	160
• Telephones	160
• Mail	162
• Conclusion	163
Further Reading	**165**
Index	**166**
Acknowledgments	**168**

Map of Slovenia

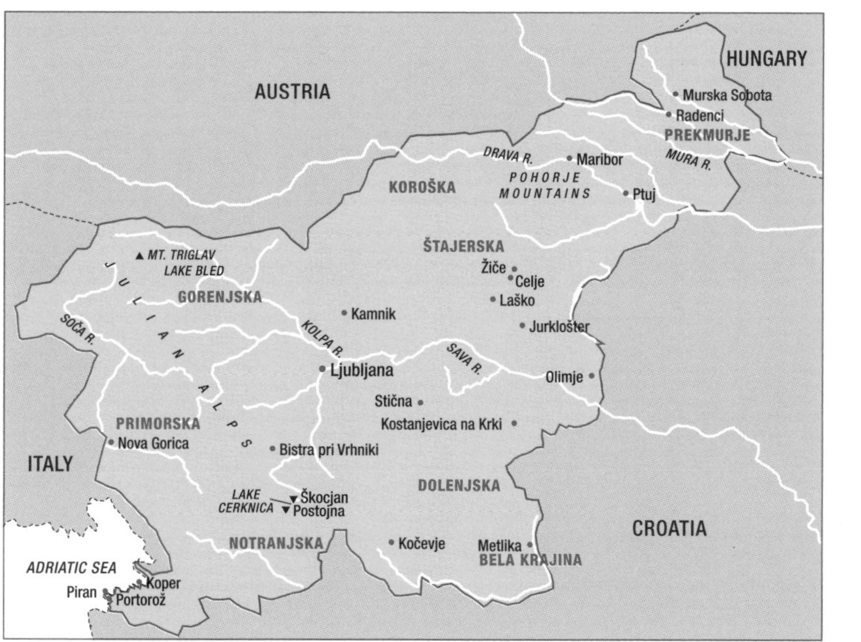

introduction

Slovenia is like the fortunate solution to a brain teaser where the goal was to pack as much history and geography as possible into a relatively small space. The country is beautiful beyond belief: rolling hills stretch eastward into plains, and northwest to majestic Alpine vistas. Throw in an Adriatic coastline and the unique Karst landscape, and you have much of Europe in a thimble.

Over the centuries, the area has belonged to many kingdoms and regimes. Until Slovenians gained independence in 1991, they had sat back and watched the mighty rise and fall. Unlike other nations in the area, they never had a glorious modern kingdom encompassing all Slovenians. What is today the Republic of Slovenia includes territory divided at various times among the Habsburgs, the Venetian Republic, Hungary, and others. This is one of the reasons Slovenians look to their language, rather than a real or imagined historical golden age, as the benchmark of national identity. As far as nationhood goes, their golden age is now, in a new state in which the language of the people is, finally, also the language of government.

For centuries, Slovenians were looked down upon as Slavic underlings. Then, in ex-Yugoslavia, they were regarded by their Balkan neighbors as being eerily Austrian—a cold, reserved Alpine people with an addiction to work, and perhaps a mild aversion to fun. Though this opinion was not held without a sense of humor and even a certain amount of respect, the stereotypes are hard to shake, and many Slovenians label themselves as melancholic, morose, or introverted.

For lack of a better term, this is the lesser, public Slovenia, where there is no rush to greet you, where bureaucrats are stony faced, and where people knock into you on the street without apology. What some see as coldness, even a dash of rudeness, is often part of a pragmatic and sincere reserve: there is no need to flash fake smiles just because you have some minor paperwork to take care of, or pretend remorse if the bump was accidental and minor.

The private Slovenia, the world of family, friends, and close acquaintances, is a different place altogether, and if the above stereotypes were overstated for the public Slovenia, they are entirely absent from the private one. This other Slovenia, peopled of course by the same individuals, is a realm of amazing generosity, intimacy, and honesty.

Given the splendor of the natural surroundings, the country's resilience through the centuries, and its successes since 1991, the Slovenians' modesty is remarkable. Even more remarkable in light of their history of being ruled by others is their habit of treating their Western visitors much more warmly and kindly than they treat their own countrymen and women.

Key Facts

Official Name	Republic of Slovenia (Republika Slovenija)	Seceded from Yugoslavia 1991; joined the European Union 2004
Capital City	Ljubljana (pop. 263,000)	
Major City	Maribor (pop. 110,000)	
Area	7,827 sq. miles (20,273 sq. km)	
Borders	Italy, Austria, Hungary, Croatia	
Climate	Alpine, Continental, Mediterranean	
Currency	Euro	Adopted in 2007
Population	2,032,362	Density: 160 per sq. mile (100 per sq. km)
Ethnic Makeup	83.1 percent Slovenian	Recognized Italian and Hungarian minorities
Language	Slovenian (also called Slovene); Italian in the coastal area; Hungarian in the northeast	
Religion	Primarily Roman Catholic (approx. 60%); small (1%) but historically important Evangelical minority; some 30 other registered churches. Some state support	
Government	Two-chamber parliamentary democracy, consisting of the National Assembly (90 deputies, including 1 each representing the Hungarian and Italian minorities) and the National Council (40 members). The president is the head of state, the prime minister the head of government.	

Media	Two national public TV channels (Slovenia 1 and Slovenia 2) and three main private channels (Pop TV, Kanal A, and TV3). Much TV programming consists of subtitled US and UK shows.	The public "Radio Slovenija" has three main channels covering news (Ra SLO 1), popular culture (Val 202), and high culture (Ars). Radio Slovenia International frequently broadcasts in English.
Press	Eight daily newspapers: *Delo* is the leading broadsheet, *Slovenske novice* the leading tabloid.	*The Slovenia Times* appears monthly in English.
Electricity	230 volts, 50 Hz	UK appliances require a continental adaptor; US and Canadian appliances also need transformers.
TV, Video, and DVD	PAL B	DVDs are Region 2, and do not work on US players.
Internet Domain	.si	
Telephone	Country code: 386	For international calls, dial 00; for local calls, dial 0 before the number
Time Zone	GMT/UTC +1	Slovenia has daylight saving time.

chapter **one**

LAND & PEOPLE

GEOGRAPHY

Slovenia's natural beauty is astonishing, and it would be more accurate to speak of the country's natural *beauties*. A Slovenian legend has it that when God was allotting nature's bounty, he initially forgot this country. His last-minute solution was to take bits of the best from other places: gorgeous Alpine ranges, the less craggy Pohorje Mountains, the Pannonian plain stretching toward Hungary, hill after hill rolling southward into the horizon, the unique Karst landscape, rivers aplenty, and a few miles of Adriatic coastline. There's even a disappearing body of water here—for much of the year Lake Cerknica is dry but, come the spring rains, the basin fills to become a massive, shallow lake.

The fourth-smallest of the twenty-seven European Union states, Slovenia is half the size of Switzerland and almost exactly the size of Massachusetts or Wales. Driving from any border to any other border of Slovenia takes about three hours.

A political map of Slovenia looks like a running chicken: Prekmurje, in the northeast, is the head and beak that poke into Hungary; the Alpine northwest contains the tail feathers, and the Adriatic region forms the hind leg. More than half of the chicken is colored a pleasant green by the abundant forests, and traveling in by air offers a stunning view of both verdant and Alpine terrains.

Slovenia is bordered by Italy, Austria, Hungary, Croatia, and about twenty-five miles (43 km) of the Adriatic coast, which makes for an astounding degree of regional, cultural, and geographical variety. The seaside town of Piran looks like an extension of Venice, and a day spent strolling its narrow, winding streets will give you a completely different picture from a day spent in Maribor, near the Austrian border, or in Murska Sobota, near Hungary.

There are four main geographical regions in Slovenia: the Alpine region, which extends over

40 percent of Slovenian territory and includes Mount Triglav (9,396 feet, or 2,396 m), the fertile and densely populated Pannonian plain, the southern Karst region that rests on porous limestone, and the Slovenian Littoral near the Adriatic Sea.

The traditional names for the individual regions include Gorenjska (Upper Carniola), Štajerska (Styria), Prekmurje (for the lands beyond the Mura River), Koroška (Carinthia), Notranjska (Inner Carniola), Dolenjska (Lower Carniola), Bela Krajina (White Carniola), and Primorska (the area "by the sea"). These names are derived for the most part from the German labels the Habsburg rulers slapped on their crown lands in present-day Slovenia. In spite of this dubious heritage, Slovenians identify most strongly with these traditional regions. Many insist on using the Slovenian designations even in English texts, and so it is that visitors will see "Koroška" at least as often as "Carinthia."

Fresh water is abundant in Slovenia, and in addition to the many underground springs there are dozens of rivers crisscrossing the country. The largest of these is the Sava, which starts as a trickle at the Savica Falls in the Julian Alps, and grows and grows as it makes its way south. Other major rivers are the Drava and Mura, whose waters cross the Austrian-Slovenian border before converging in Croatia. The clear Alpine waters of the Soča River—better known as the Isonzo River of First World War infamy—wind among lovely mountain scenery near the Italian border. On the opposite side of Slovenia is the equally picturesque Kolpa River, which forms seventy miles (113 km) of the border with Croatia.

CLIMATE

In Slovenia you can have a late-season Alpine ski in the morning and then head to the beach in Piran or Portorož for an early-season dip. The difference in temperature is only partly determined by elevation, because any description of Slovenia's climate must first specify *which Slovenia*. There are three climatic regions, and traveling just a few dozen miles may take you into a different weather zone as blue skies suddenly darken and the temperature drops.

The Adriatic coast is blessed with a Mediterranean climate of warm summers and mild winters. The port city of Koper, for example, has an average winter temperature well above freezing. However, Koper and the rest of the Primorska region pay for this winter mildness with the *Burja* (Bora), a biting wind that can reach 120 mph (200 kmph).

Most of Slovenia has a continental climate, with cold winters and hot summers. The average winter temperature in Ljubljana, Maribor, and Murska Sobota hovers just below the freezing point, and the average summer temperature is approximately 70°F (20°C). Heat waves are a given in any summer, but there is usually a welcome overnight breeze to help bring the mercury down.

In the Alps the temperature is always significantly cooler than in the lowlands. The average year-round temperature measured at the meteorological station at Kredarica (elevation 8,250 feet, or 2,515 m) below Mount Triglav is below the freezing point.

Precipitation in Slovenia averages just below five inches (125 mm) in January, and a little above five inches (135 mm) in July. Flooding, especially in the fall, is not uncommon.

THE PEOPLE

On a clear day, the view from Mount Triglav extends to almost all areas that are or once were Slovenian lands, including the still existing Slovenian communities in Italy and Austria. The Republic of Slovenia has approximately two million inhabitants, of which the overwhelming majority (83 percent) are ethnically Slovenian. However, many Slovenians may have an Austrian great-grandmother, a Croatian uncle, or an Italian aunt, and so on.

There are two traditional minorities of Italians and Hungarians in the border regions, numbering approximately 4,000 and 8,000 respectively. In acknowledgment of their centuries-long presence, the Constitution grants official language status "in those municipalities where Italian or Hungarian national communities reside . . . ." In addition to bilingual schools and signs, the law guarantees a set amount of radio and television programming in Italian and Hungarian. While these communities preserve their cultural and linguistic heritage, they are well integrated into Slovenian society. Similarly, there are some 180,000 ethnic Slovenians living in Austria, Italy, and Hungary.

Predictably, there is also a strong Croatian presence in border regions, and mixed marriages are frequent. The closer you get to the frontier, the harder it is to discern who is speaking a Croatian-flavored Slovenian dialect and who a Slovenian-flavored Croatian dialect.

The German-speaking population, including those in the ancient settlements in and around Kočevje (German "Gottschee"), dwindled away during the twentieth century, dropping to nil after the Second World War. The original group came to the region in the fourteenth century, diligently carved out an existence from the heavily forested terrain, built villages, and, living in linguistic isolation, developed their own dialect over time.

One other traditional minority deserves mention: there is a tiny community of Serbians in the southwest region of Bela Krajina. Originally settlers fleeing Ottoman rule in 1526, they established four villages and have maintained an archaic type of Serbian to the present, along with a penchant for handcrafting traditional shirts.

Today, major groups include about 4,000 Roma, or Gypsies—some of whose ancestors arrived in the fifteenth century—as well as Albanians and other immigrants from the former Yugoslavia. Slovenians often point out that integration is less obvious with these groups—something visitors may not notice.

Ljubljana (pop. 263,000) and Maribor (pop. 110,000) are the two large cities, and only half of the population in Slovenia is truly urban. Most people live in one of the hundreds of smaller towns and villages. As far as values and attitudes go, the division between city and country is not great, and Ljubljana is not radically more open and liberal than most midsized towns. Beyond rabid soccer rivalries, regional animosity is more playful than visceral.

Beyond Europe, there are large Slovenian minorities living in the United States, Canada, Australia, and Argentina. These communities are keeping traditions alive through church activities, newspapers, language classes, and the not-so-occasional picnic or daylong party complete with pig roast. In Argentina, many third-generation Slovenians still speak the language without ever having visited their ancestral country.

A BRIEF HISTORY

"Finally!" sums up Slovenia's progression from nation to state, as their history is one of resilience and patience. Slovenia gained independence in 1991, after seven hundred years of toil under the Habsburgs, and several decades under Yugoslav rule. In each case, they had a homeland but no state of their own. That this relatively small nation was not swallowed up by Germanic or a neighboring Slavic culture is remarkable.

Before Slovenians

There is much evidence of human habitation that predates the sixth-century arrival of the Slavic tribes. The earliest remains date from prehistory and include a few implements as well as what appears to be a Neanderthal flute crafted from a bear's femur. Though experts quibble over whether this forty-thousand-year-old artifact is really a musical instrument, the former femur portends a rich cultural tradition.

During the Bronze Age (2000 to 900 BCE), settlers lived in the marshy surroundings of what is today Ljubljana, building houses on stilts to keep their feet dry. In the eighth century BCE Illyrian tribes swept through this area. Four centuries later Celtic tribes came all the way from France and Germany, mixing with the locals and establishing the kingdom of Noricum. The names of the Sava and Drava rivers, as well as the lovely Alpine surroundings of Bohinj, are derived from Celtic roots.

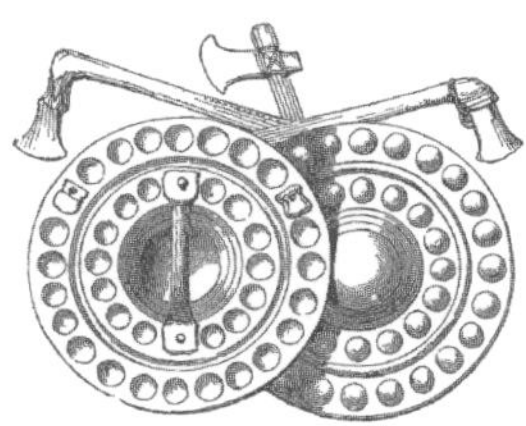

The Romans arrived in the second century BCE, initially trading with the Celts, then battling them, and finally assimilating in the newly established provinces of Pannonia and Noricum. The many Roman ruins that remain in the cities of Emona (Ljubljana), Celeia (Celje), and Poetovio (Ptuj) are all part of the *via gemina* that leads eastward to Hungary.

Under pressure from the barbarians, Rome abandoned the area at the end of the fourth century CE, and Huns, Ostrogoths, and Langobards stormed through these parts in the fifth and sixth centuries, sacking and plundering as they pleased. The Langobards made their collective way into Italy in 568, crossing the Julian Alps in the style of Hannibal.

Slavs and Slovenians

At some time in the sixth century Slavic tribes arrived from the Carpathian Basin. They traveled westward toward the Alps and the Karst landscape, and eventually absorbed the Roman, Celtic, and Illyrian cultures.

A large east-Alpine Slavic state that stretched perhaps as far as Leipzig in present-day Germany was soon established under King Samo, but this federation disintegrated after his death in 658. Slavs from this once formidable kingdom succumbed to Bavarian and Magyar attacks. Cut off from other Slavs, the Alpine Slavs began to develop a distinct language and culture.

The history of the Slovenians as a people dates from around the time of Samo's death, and the pre-Slovenian Duchy of Carantania was soon established at Krn Castle by the Holy Roman Emperor Otto I. (This is now Karnburg, just north of Klagenfurt, in Austria). This Duchy is of symbolic importance because it marked the first Slovenian "state."

It also played host to a rather democratic ceremony: whenever wealthy commoners confirmed a new nobleman as their leader, a peasant would perch on the "Prince's Stone" (*knježji kamen*). He would not budge until the chosen one publicly swore his allegiance to the people and pledged to act on their behalf. Details about the ceremony are sketchy, but it is known to have been carried out in a Slavic language. Slovenia opted to use the Prince's Stone to adorn the obverse side of their two-cent piece when it joined the Eurozone in 2007. This bothered some Austrians, who pointed out that the Prince's Stone had long been housed in a museum in Klagenfurt, before being moved to the provincial parliament there in 2005.

The Middle Ages (500-1500)

Carantania remains a powerful symbol, not least because for centuries Slovenian statehood remained a dream. After the supremacy of the Franks, Slovenia fell to Germanic lands, and the history of division begins: Slovenia became the marks, or crown lands, of Carniola, Carinthia, and Styria.

Slovenia converted to Christianity during the eighth century and was later controlled from Salzburg and the Patriarchate of Aquileia near the city of Udine in northeastern Italy. The latter, especially, gained great secular power over time. More significantly for Slovenian cultural history, the religious texts that make up the Freising Manuscripts date from the late tenth or early eleventh century. Written on parchment, these three short texts are translations from Latin and German sources and represent the earliest preserved instance of Slovenian.

During medieval times, Slovenian nobles lost out to German counts, and peasants became serfs in the feudal system. This loss in social status did bring them to the West, a legacy still obvious in Yugoslavia, where Slovenia (along with Croatia) was more developed when it came to education and trade.

Between the tenth and thirteenth centuries a number of monasteries were established in Slovenian lands, the most important being the Carthusian monasteries at Bistra, Žiče, and Jurklošter, and the Cistercian monasteries at Kostanjevica na Krki and Stična. Long before the

first central European universities were founded, these were leading educational centers in which many languages flourished. Some manuscripts produced in these places include marginal notes written in Slovenian—evidence, perhaps, of the Catholic Church's early role in preserving Slovenian identity.

After the defeat of Ottokar II, King of Bohemia and Margrave of Moravia, by Rudolf of Habsburg in 1278, centuries of Habsburg rule over Slovenians began. Habsburg hegemony over the Slovenian lands, however, was not obvious from the start and was only solidified in subsequent decades and centuries thanks to the family's knack of marrying well and wisely.

By the early fifteenth century, the Counts of Celje were acting as a counterbalance to the

Habsburgs. They had acquired much land around Celje and elsewhere in present-day Slovenia, and soon they were no longer beholden to the Habsburgs; they established a court and took on the aspect of an independent state. Unfortunately for them, they were less successful than the Habsburgs at marrying, and even weaker at producing robust male offspring. The family line ended in Belgrade in 1456 when Ulrich II, in town to help defend against the Turks, was murdered at the command of Hungarian noblemen with a score to settle. Despite their Germanic heritage, the Counts remain a key symbol of Slovenia—and the three yellow stars rising above the image of Mount Triglav on the Slovenian flag attest to this.

As the Middle Ages waned, Slovenia suffered Turkish raids, albeit not as often as its eastern neighbors. Unlike Hungary and Croatia, Slovenia was never under Ottoman rule. Turkish figures appear—always nefariously—in Slovenian folk and literary tales. In the story of Martin Krpan, for example, the simple Slovenian peasant travels to Vienna, where he saves the Empire by slaying the giant Brdavs, an obvious representation of Turkish marauders.

Reformation and Counter-Reformation

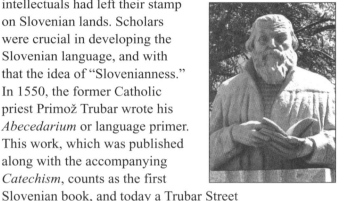

The Protestant Reformation prepared the way for Slovenian literary culture. Although Protestantism quickly succumbed to Catholicism after the Counter-Reformation, Protestant intellectuals had left their stamp on Slovenian lands. Scholars were crucial in developing the Slovenian language, and with that the idea of "Slovenianness." In 1550, the former Catholic priest Primož Trubar wrote his *Abecedarium* or language primer. This work, which was published along with the accompanying *Catechism*, counts as the first Slovenian book, and today a Trubar Street can be found in every town.

Between the sixteenth and eighteenth centuries, there was also great displeasure with the protective but tax-hungry Habsburg rulers, and a series of peasant revolts marked the era. Slovenians fondly evoke these unsuccessful revolts as acts of national resistance.

Napoleon

Napoleon is well viewed in Slovenia, and downtown Ljubljana boasts a tall monument to his Illyrian Provinces. These Provinces, which extended far down the Dalmatian coast in present-day Croatia, were established as an autonomous region of the French Empire in 1809. This entailed yet another division of Slovenia, as the western parts of the homeland were added to the Provinces, while other parts remained Austrian lands. Napoleon's immediate objective was to block Austria's access to the Adriatic Sea. The benefits to Slovenians were obvious at once: education was now in the language of the land, and Slovenians could thus receive schooling in their mother tongue. Official business was also in Slovenian for a change, which meant that unilingual Germans could no longer administer the locals. The experiment did not last long, and with the defeat of Napoleon in 1814 these lands again became Austrian, but the principles of the Revolution took root.

Linguistic Awakening

The nineteenth century saw, if not a full-scale national awakening, then at least a linguistic awakening. The national poet France Prešeren, whose statue stands guard over Ljubljana's main square, was born in 1800 and died in 1849, just one year after the revolutionary fervor of 1848. Prešeren was a true Romantic patriot, and his libationary and pacifistic *Zdravljica* ("A Toast") is now the national anthem. In Janko Lavrin's translation, it reads:

God's blessing on all nations,
Who long and work for that bright day,
When o'er earth's habitations
No war, no strife shall hold its sway;
Who long to see
That all men free
No more shall foes, but neighbors be.

That Slovenians' language survived centuries of Habsburg rule, even before the rise of national poet France Prešeren, is extraordinary. For much of its history Slovenian was primarily a spoken language and thus lacked the credentials and bragging rights of a literary language. In the nineteenth century, secondary and higher education was in German; going to university generally meant traveling to Vienna and writing in a foreign language. Thus, German exerted a strong influence on formal written Slovenian.

In 1808, Jernej Kopitar codified Slovenian by publishing the first scholarly grammar (Adam Bohorič had written one in Latin back in 1584). Kopitar, along with other scholars who followed, strove to purify the language of Germanisms and generally Slavicize it. "Better a borrowed or old-fashioned Slavic word or structure than that of the oppressor" was the motto.

In 1848 a political nationalism of sorts emerged, and the first calls were articulated for *Zedinjena Slovenija* (Unified Slovenia). Rather than aspiring to outright independence and a state of their own, the Slovenes wanted to form a province within the Habsburg monarchy, with Slovenian as an official language. As everywhere else in Europe's Spring of Nations, this attempt at national self-determination failed.

In 1867, Slovenia was divided yet again, this time into the newly formed Austro-Hungarian monarchy. The northeastern region of Prekmurje fell to the Hungarians, and most of the rest of Slovenia to the Austrian half of the double monarchy.

As the twentieth century approached, Slovenians asserted themselves more and more as a cultural and economic force. Cities like Ljubljana, which had been German in flavor, became Slovenian. The Slovenian middle class was on the rise, and soon Slovenians had their own mercantile institutions and more Slovenians had won the right to vote. The first Slovenian political parties sprang to life in the 1890s, and if the Catholic-influenced Slovenian People's Party and the Socialists did not share a political view, they were alike in their concept of the nation.

Language became a central political issue, one that ultimately felled a shaky coalition government in the capital of Vienna. Since the late 1880s liberal politicians had been securing

Slovenian votes on the promise of a few classes a week in their own language at the grammar school in Celje. When the promise was not fulfilled, the Celje Grammar School became a *cause célèbre* for similar Slavic-German struggles elsewhere in the Empire, most obviously in Bohemia. In 1895, the first classes finally commenced; the result in faraway Vienna was a breakdown of the coalition as the less liberal German-speaking politicians withdrew their support. Though the immediate aftermath was direct Imperial rule rather than parliamentary government, the events were a harbinger of the double monarchy's demise.

The First World War and a Slavic Kingdom

The First World War was as calamitous for Slovenia as it was for the rest of Europe. The battles on the Soča (Isonzo) front between Italians and those fighting under Austro-Hungary

were among the bloodiest of the war and over half a million young men lost their lives in the mountainous terrain. Slovenia remained loyal to Austria, but nascent calls for autonomy become louder after so much death.

In the territorial back-and-forth inherent in any war and its subsequent treaties, Slovenia lost much land in 1918. The Habsburg Empire was carved up. Slovenia yielded a great deal of territory to Italy and also to Austria; some of it by the volition of Slovenians themselves—there was a 1920 plebiscite in which the Slovenians living in present-day Austria decided to join that country rather than try their luck in another new state. One quarter of the Slovenian population now lived outside Slovenian lands.

After a very brief attempt at a postwar State of Slovenians, Croats and Serbs, with its capital in Zagreb, Slovenians now found themselves last and least in a new monarchy—The Kingdom of Serbs, Croats, and Slovenians. In 1929, the kingdom was renamed the Kingdom of Yugoslavia, the constitution was abolished, civil liberties were suspended, and state centralization intensified. Slovenians had little pull in the new Kingdom's capital in Belgrade, but they did enjoy linguistic and cultural freedom. In the interwar years, Slovenia prospered from continuing industrialization, and became one of the most economically vibrant parts of what is commonly referred to as "Old Yugoslavia."

However, even before the horrors of the Second World War played themselves out in the Slovenian landscape, the political landscape was messy. Catholic conservatives, anti-Church leftists, and communists battled ferociously in the turbulent 1930s.

The Second World War and Its Aftermath

In 1941, after Germany invaded and quickly subjugated the Kingdom of Yugoslavia, Slovenia was sliced up among Axis powers: Italy got the area extending from Ljubljana to the coast, Germany the center and the north, and Slovenians in Prekmurje once again found themselves in Hungarian territory.

A Liberation Front was quickly formed by various groups, led by the Communist Party of Slovenia, and they began a brave resistance movement against the Axis powers, before joining up with the Tito-led Partisans who eventually liberated Yugoslavia with the goal of establishing a communist state. At the same time as Partisans were fighting Nazis and Italian Fascists, a fierce civil war was raging between them and anticommunist Slovenians, who were favor of an independent Slovenia. These *domobranci* were thought by many to be in bed with the Nazis, and in some cases this was surely true. They had received arms from Axis powers, especially the Germans, and history does not smile kindly on such deals.

Some contemporary historians plead for nuance, arguing that it was not always a case of the good Partisans against ardent Nazis and Nazi-sympathizers and that after the war Partisan-friendly historians had a stranglehold on official history. For certain conservative Slovenian patriots, collaboration was seen as a necessary evil; others questioned the utility of resistance that would result in immoderate and deadly repercussions by the Nazis. For example, after the Partisans killed a single Nazi officer near the village of Frankolovo, the occupiers rounded up and executed one hundred Slovenian civilians.

The Second World War is easily the ugliest chapter of Slovenian history, and the horrors did not stop with the defeat of Nazi Germany. To their credit, the Partisans liberated the area of Yugoslavia by themselves, without Soviet help; to the dishonor of some Partisans, there was much bloodshed, understandable revenge, and malice after the war. As the Partisans emerged victorious in the last days of the war, thousands of Slovenians fled to Austria.

The British troops who had command over these refugees in the confusing months following the war sent some ten to twelve thousand collaborators back to Slovenia; contrary to promises made and word given, many of these were sent to a hasty death without trials in the hilly wooded area of Kočevski Rog, among other places. Only after 1991 did these grim stories officially come to light—most recently in March 2009, when hundreds of bodies were found in a mineshaft that had been sealed in concrete after the war.

Fearing execution, and doubting promises that they would be welcome in Tito's Yugoslavia, thousands of Slovenians emigrated, with much of the intelligentsia ending up in Argentina and elsewhere in the New World. Some who were children at the time of the War returned to Slovenia after the fall of Yugoslavia in the 1990s.

Communist Times

In 1943, Yugoslavia was reestablished as a socialist state under Marshal Tito, though fighting continued until 1945. The port city of Trieste, which had always had an ethnically mixed population, reverted to Italy in 1954 after a brief occupation by Partisans near the war's end. For the three years immediately following the war, Slovenia and the rest of the Socialist Federal Republic of Yugoslavia were philosophically aligned with Stalin. In 1948 Tito and Stalin split, leading the way to a less harsh path for the socialist republics of Bosnia and Herzegovina, Croatia, Macedonia, Montenegro, Serbia, and Slovenia that made up the Yugoslav state.

While Tito's Yugoslavia was not without its show trials, work camps, and mini-gulags, it became more market-oriented and Western than the hard-line communism experienced to the east. Rather than hiding behind the Iron Curtain, Tito argued for a middle path, and it was in Yugoslavia that the Non-Aligned Movement was created, a movement that tried to steer between blocs in the Cold War.

Slovenia was easily the most prosperous of the six Yugoslav republics, and much money generated in Slovenia was funneled to the capital in Belgrade to help support poorer regions in the south. When the Yugoslav economy faltered greatly after the death of Tito in 1980, Slovenians became more frustrated than ever with such transfer payments. A mass democrat movement pushed the Slovenian Communist party in the direction of democratic reform. Confrontation grew with the Serbian communist party led by Slobodan Milošević.

Postcommunist Times

In late spring 1990, when the fall of Yugoslavia already seemed imminent, Slovenia held free elections. The Democratic Opposition of Slovenia (DEMOS coalition) won 55 percent of the votes, over parties composed mainly of representatives of the old regime. Lojze Peterle, who was chief of the Slovenian Christian Democrats, was elected Prime Minister, while the crafty and widely respected Milan Kučan, who had headed the Slovenian communists in Yugoslav times, became President. Slovenia's subsequent calls for a radical reconstruction of the Yugoslav Federation fell on deaf ears in Belgrade. In December of that year a referendum was held to determine whether voters wanted an independent Slovenia. They did, and more than 90 percent voted "Yes."

On June 25 1991, Slovenia seceded. The Ten-Day-War ensued as the mighty Yugoslavian Army attacked. As the name of this short war indicates, the Yugoslav Army soon retreated, and by November 1991 there were no more Yugoslav soldiers in Slovenia. It was difficult to argue that ethnically homogeneous Slovenia, with a clearly different language from that of its neighbors within Yugoslavia, belonged to any of the other republics. Germany, Austria, and the Vatican were quick to recognize the new state. This proved to be a dangerous precedent of establishing new states on the basis of perceived ethnicity, and the stage was set for bloodier conflict throughout ex-Yugoslavia. Even as battles raged just over the eastern and southern borders, Slovenia began a march toward the European Union. It was as if these latest European wars were thousands of miles away.

Relatively unhindered by the war, with a fairly stable economy and political system, Slovenia again looked to its historical partners in Western Europe. It entered both NATO and the European Union in 2004, and on January 1, 2007, Slovenia gave up its young currency known as the *tolar* in favor of the Euro. From January to June 2008, Slovenia became the first postcommunist state to hold the rotating presidency of the Council of the European Union.

GOVERNMENT

Slovenia is a democratic republic, with a Constitution dating from December 1991. The Constitution establishes the division of legislative, executive, and judicial powers. It also literally lays down the laws for Slovenia's parliamentary system and entrenches the fact that Slovenia is a welfare or "social state."

The National Assembly, or lower house, which elects the prime minister, consists of ninety members of parliament. This number includes two representatives (one each) from the Italian and Hungarian minorities. Forty of the ninety MPs are directly elected in a "winner takes all" race, and the remaining fifty are selected from party lists on the basis of proportional representation; a political party's threshold for entering parliament is 4 percent. Slovenia has fixed election dates, with a fall election every four years.

In purely mathematical terms, each MP represents a mere twenty thousand citizens (approximately one-fifth of the number an MP represents in most Anglophone lands, and one-thirtieth of the number in the USA). Some say that Slovenia is swimming in MPs. However, because the state/provincial level does not exist in Slovenia, there are only two levels of government. This leads to a very centralized system, and the federal level concerns itself with such matters as education and civil law.

The National Council is a forty-member advisory board. Intended as a counterbalance to party politics, it is composed of individuals who represent various social, business, and professional, as well as local or regional, concerns. Members are not full-time politicians, in the belief that this will enable them to maintain closer contact with the sectors they represent. Council members are indirectly elected by groups speaking for employers, employees, farmers, tradesmen, independent professions, and noncommercial realms, as well as local interests.

The president is the head of state and the commander-in-chief of the armed forces, and is also responsible for promulgating laws. He (to date, all presidents and prime ministers have been male) is directly elected for a period of five years, and can serve a maximum of two terms. The presidential role is more akin to that of the British monarch than that of the man in the White House.

The National Assembly adopts laws, budgets, and treaties, and performs all the usual legislative business of a democracy. As well, it appoints the president of the government and constitutional court judges.

Slovenia has seven of the 736 seats in the European Parliament and, like all small EU states, is thus well represented in relation to its population.

POLITICS

If multiparty systems are a sign of a healthy democracy, Slovenia has successfully made the transformation from a de facto one-party system to a robust democracy since independence in 1991. In 2011 there were seven parties in parliament, four of which were part of the governing coalition. Election turnout ranges between a respectable 60 percent and 70 percent for national elections, and a dismal 30 percent for European Parliament elections (both numbers are near the European average).

The leading parties in 2011 are the left-leaning Social Democrats (SD) and the right-leaning Slovenian Democratic Party (SDS). In recent years each of these parties has enjoyed approximately 30 percent of the popular vote, meaning that coalition governments are the norm. The future of DeSUS (the Democratic Party of

Pensioners of Slovenia) looks rosy because the population is fast aging. More importantly, DeSUS has proven to be kingmakers in the past two elections, switching from a right-of-center to a left-of-center coalition.

The need for a coalition is useful for political parties that have faded. The once mighty Liberal Democracy of Slovenia (LDS), that governed for much of the young state's history, fell into the fringe territory of 5 percent, a whisker below the right-wing populist Slovenian National Party (SNS). The LDS's decline was accelerated by fearsome infighting and the establishing of new left-wing parties such as the cutely named "Zares," which translates as "for real." Divisions have also occurred on the right, as the Christian People's Party of New Slovenia (NSi) has, at least temporarily, dropped off the political map. They, too, saw the formation of a breakaway party.

Voting patterns are fragmented throughout the country—that is, there is no guarantee that the left will win some areas or towns, and the right in others. The general assumption among all major parties is that the welfare state model is positive but too costly.

Politicians are not held in very high esteem in Slovenia. Their salaries are fairly high, and the basic pay for a Slovenian member of the European Parliament approaches that of his colleague from pricy Luxembourg or Sweden, and is approximately twice that of a Spanish representative (though it is far below that of Greece, Germany, Austria, and several others).

Corruption among politicians is omnipresent in the media and town square gossip. That said, few politicians have ever been prosecuted. For the past few years, Slovenia has been placed a respectable twenty-sixth or twenty-seventh on Transparency International's Corruption Index, which seems to contradict the widespread accusations of political corruption. This ranking puts Slovenia well ahead of all its neighbors (with the exception of Austria) and ties it with Estonia for the lead among former communist countries.

On a positive note, even the highest-level cabinet ministers make themselves generously available for lengthy print and television interviews. Politicians are often minor celebrities, sharing cover space with screen idols on the covers of glossy magazines. The popular press follows their amorous dalliances and personal lives rather benevolently, and it is hard to imagine a Monicagate happening in Slovenia.

ECONOMIC TRANSFORMATION

Three factors aided Slovenia's relatively smooth transition to the open market after 1991: Yugoslavia was far more market-oriented than other communist states, Slovenia had a centuries-long tradition of trade with the West, and Slovenia was the most economically developed region of Yugoslavia (along with northern Croatia). Nevertheless, after the Second World War most of Slovenia's trade had been within Yugoslavia, and the demise of Yugoslavia meant the loss of these markets. While Croatia remains a strong trading partner, other EU countries—most notably, Germany, Italy, and France—are now the key markets.

Partly as a result of strict laws governing foreign ownership, Slovenia did not see the rampant foreign takeovers common in other postcommunist central European states in the 1990s. This, however, is changing, and one sees more foreign control as the years go by. Although one hears often of the elixir of privatization, there is profound state control or interest in many companies.

Like all other Western economies, Slovenia is continuing the shift toward the so-called service economy, and industrial and manufacturing sectors are in decline. Agriculture represents a mere 2 percent of the GDP. Aside from insurance, banking, and other financial services, the largest Slovenian companies are involved in energy production and distribution. Other important industries are pharmaceuticals, breweries, and the manufacturing of household appliances to keep the Slovenian beer cold.

chapter **two**

VALUES & ATTITUDES

Even if the times are not a-changin' as briskly as they were immediately after independence in 1991, Slovenia remains a country in transition. Half a decade in the European Union, along with the inevitable effects of globalization, has made Slovenia a less traditional Central European state than it was even a few years ago under communism. Shopping malls parade the same goods as in Toronto, the kids dress like young people in Chicago, and the euro is the currency that much of Europe uses. Yet certain traits remain. These include a Germanic love of cleanliness and order, pragmatism, a quiet conservatism, moderation in almost everything, and a solid work ethic.

SMALL AND WESTERN

Territorial smallness is omnipresent in the Slovenian mind. You will often overhear "*Slovenija je majhna država*" ("Slovenia is a small country") in conversation, and Slovenian newspapers regularly refer to it. Sometimes it is mentioned to highlight the challenges of working in a small business world or small market, and sometimes to emphasize the latest sporting achievements against larger nations. In a region of the world scarred by Hitler and Mussolini's megalomania, as well as Balkan leaders' delusions of grandeur, this appreciation of the petite is refreshing. There is a Swiss-like self-satisfaction throughout Slovenia. The country is as beautiful as it is small, and they wouldn't want it any other way.

Slovenians adamantly emphasize that their country belongs to Central Europe, is not part of the Balkans, and is definitely not Slovakia. In geographical, historical, and geological terms, Slovenia has always been closer to Austria and Italy than to the south Slavic states. This is as much a question of values and mentality and—yes—pride as it is a political or geographical concern. Slovenians see themselves as more punctual, harder working, more developed, more market-oriented, and less volatile, but also less sanguine than their former compatriots in Yugoslavia.

IDENTITY—DEFINED BY LANGUAGE

Who is a Slovenian? A Slovenian is a fluent speaker of Slovenian. In other words, Slovenians define themselves through language rather than through blood, history, or citizenship. This is partly because their language is so clearly different from the other languages of ex-Yugoslavia (not to speak of Italian, German, and Hungarian, which are not in the same language group), partly because many

Slovenians live beyond the country's borders, and partly because there is a quiet assumption that only those with an ethnic claim to being Slovenian actually speak the language.

Slovenians' linguistic concerns are always identity concerns, and their obsession with language is therefore understandable. This manifests itself in various ways: there are fierce intellectual debates over whether it is acceptable to use the English "Styria" for the region of "Štajerska," or "Carinthia" for "Koroška"—that is, over whether this constitutes a veiled land claim; letters to the newspaper and comments on Internet forums complain that Serbian and other languages from former Yugoslavia are crowding out Slovenian on the streets of Ljubljana; at least one writer has quipped that where the English talk about the weather, Slovenians fill conversation gaps with musings on the state of their language and the threat of its extinction.

RELIGION

Whenever Slovenians speak positively or negatively of Church or religion, they really mean Catholicism, since Slovenia is overwhelmingly Roman Catholic in terms of religious affiliation, cultural tradition, and influence. The cultural reach of the Church is obvious everywhere in Slovenia, and this influence is best seen in architectural and geographical terms—from any valley in Slovenia, you will see up to half a dozen hilltop churches and chapels dotting the landscape. This cultural presence was not lost on the Vatican in January 1992, when it became one of the first states formally to recognize Slovenia's independence (the Holy See recognized Croatia, another traditionally Catholic country, at the same time).

If one associates public piety, ostentatious ceremony, emotionality, and a generally laid-back approach to work with Catholicism, Slovenia is not overtly Catholic. On the other hand, Slovenians excel at guilt, are very close with the family, especially the mother, and they have a love-hate relationship with hierarchy. This is surely a reflection of the Catholic past. On a more culinary and quotidian level, also non-pious Slovenians eat traditional foods at Easter and refrain from mowing the lawn on Sundays, the day of rest.

Slovenians generally keep their religious views to themselves. They may go to church on Sunday, but they will not yap about it on Monday, which is a pragmatic attitude for a country in which religion is a taboo topic. It is a taboo because ever since the rise of party politics in Slovenia before the First World War, religion has been highly politicized in Slovenia. Years of communist rule exacerbated this. Today, nonreligious Slovenians assume that all Catholics are rampant, intolerant right-wingers, while many Slovenian Catholics consider "liberal" to be a code word for "atheist."

About 1 percent of Slovenia's population is Protestant, and this community is clustered primarily in the northeast of the country, near the Hungarian border. Inheritors of the short-lived Reformation, this group has been of great historical import to Slovenia (see page 27). Postwar historians have continually glorified this spirit of rebellion.

As a result of substantial immigration from other Yugoslav republics during the Tito era, today there are some 47,000 (primarily Bosnian) Muslims in Slovenia. They are tolerated as a religious group—but only just. There is also a substantial Serbian Orthodox population of approximately the same size as the growing Muslim population, again consisting mostly of migrants from the former Yugoslavia. This faith has a longer tradition in Slovenia, as groups of Serbian Orthodox Christians have been living in the area of Bela Krajina, near the Croatian border, for almost five centuries.

Even before the Second World War, Slovenia was home to just a few hundred Jews. Though there are remnants of a Jewish quarter in the city of Maribor, as well as a Židovska ulica (Jewish Street) in the heart of Ljubljana, there is only a nominal Jewish community in Slovenia, and many Slovenians think there are no Jews in the country at all.

AFTER COMMUNISM

The remnants of a communist society in Slovenia are less evident than elsewhere in the so-called New Europe. No ghostly Stalinesque architecture looms over Maribor or Ljubljana. Though not perfect and not without its breadlines, Yugoslav-style communism was gentler and more market-oriented than that exercised behind the Iron Curtain. You could even buy Western goods, if you were willing to pay vastly inflated customs charges. Some Slovenians argue that they fared very well during Yugoslavia because the rulers in distant Belgrade left this productive, docile, and linguistically unique republic alone. Slovenians toiled away, perhaps muttering under their breath, but never taking to the streets in protest. People regularly mention Tito, but even those who remember him fondly look back with an ironic smile rather than genuine longing.

There is little nostalgia for the socialist days of yore, when everybody had a job for life and crime and graffiti rates were lower. The concepts of left and right may continue to dominate political talk in a manner that evokes the Cold War, but all the main parties are more or less centrist and their policies do not always clearly reflect “socialist” or “capitalist” leanings. Yearnings for the past exist as airy references to "socialist tradition" and "solidarity" that are rarely translated into anything obviously ideological. However, Slovenians do retain firm ideas of what the state should pay for, and debates over the partial privatization of health care, paying for university-level education, and the handling of pensions are fierce. This occasionally turns into a matter of principle: otherwise generous Slovenians would rather lose a toe than pay for something work-related out of their own pocket. Westerners may find this sense of entitlement as odd as Slovenians find the concept of paying for health care.

BUREAUCRACY AND ATTITUDES TOWARD AUTHORITY

The recent communist past is only partially to blame for the gargantuan Slovenian bureaucracy, since Slovenians lived under the paper-happy Habsburgs long before Tito arrived on the scene. Such a history cannot be swept clear in a day. Bureaucracy is without a doubt the worst aspect of life in Slovenia. It is omnipresent, intrusive, and always accompanied by waves of forms and paperwork that threaten to submerge Slovenians and visitors alike. Slovenians look on this mass of paperwork with bemusement and only mild frustration, convinced that resistance is useless. Bureaucracy is nothing to get worked up over, nothing to fear, and not worth trying to grasp since procedures change frequently. Because the form-filling and rubber-stamping stretch into eternity—a tax refund can take ten years—simply producing evidence of having started the process usually suffices. At the same time, the Slovenian paper mill can be strangely efficient, capable of issuing passports and other documents within two days.

The dual history of Habsburg and communist structures can also be seen in the fatalistic acceptance of authority. The foreign visitor is less likely to notice this in the workplace than when dealing with employees of the local administrative office, hospital, or bank. The one in control is the one who wields the stamp, and he or she is always aware of his or her sliver of power. Expect a frosty reception when requesting information from public institutions, and even when conducting run-of-the-mill banking operations. Don't think it's because you are foreign; if anything, English speakers receive preferential treatment! Matters are improving, since just a few years ago administrative crustiness was the rule, not the exception.

SELF-IMAGE

Slovenians are both unassuming and remarkably self-deprecating. They do not toot their own horn, and positive characteristics like "hardworking" or "calm" may be morphed into "we work too hard" or "we are repressed." A Slovenian government Web site managed to work the following words and phrases into a short description of the Slovenian character: "jealous," prone to "alcoholism" and "moodiness," "submissive," "introverted," "pessimistic," "intolerant," "melancholic," and "suicidal." A foreigner can live in Slovenia for years without running into some of these national shortcomings, but that is of no matter to the Slovenians' collective sense of self. Slovenians do not take these self-labels to heart, however, and do not wallow in self-pity.

WHAT DO YOU THINK OF US?

Slovenians are perfectionists who are fascinated by what other people think of them, and this curiosity is not mere fishing for compliments. They genuinely want to know how they can improve an already delightful society.

If Slovenia appears in the English-language press, it will not escape the attention of watchful Slovenian readers, who have been taught by history to sniff out condescension. Slovenia spent centuries being governed by others, working as *hlapci* (or serfs) for foreign taskmasters, and are used to being looked down on with derision. Blame also the erroneous foreign assumption that Slovenia is underdeveloped.

Discussing what you, as an outsider, find good and bad about Slovenia makes for insightful and rewarding conversation. As long as you are marginally well-informed and express sincere interest in learning about the country, little offense will be taken.

ATTITUDE TOWARD WESTERN FOREIGNERS

In Slovenia, foreigners are not expected to fit in, mostly because Slovenians assume they will never get a grip on the language. Besides, younger Slovenians speak excellent English and have a reasonable awareness of how things work in the English-speaking world. The result is curious: many Slovenians, in particular younger ones, act differently when speaking English: they are more carefree and relaxed. Years of television in English have given them a sense of how Americans and British people behave, or are thought to behave. In fact, Slovenia must be one of the few countries to treat certain types of foreigners better than they treat each other—though this is true mostly for English-speaking Westerners. This means that fleeting conversations and transactions in English might be more pleasant than they would be in Slovenian.

TOLERANCE

Twice in recent years Slovenia has appeared on the world media stage as especially tolerant and open toward gender and racial differences—at least by Central European standards. In 2002 the transvestite act "Sestre" (Sisters) and its snappy toe tapper "Samo ljubezen" ("Only Love") was chosen to represent Slovenia at the Eurovision song contest. In truth, however, sexual orientation is a major taboo topic, and most Slovenians avoid it through pacific, quiet intolerance.

In late 2010, Peter Bossman became the "Obama of Piran" by being elected the first black mayor of a central or eastern European city. The voters spoke, the nation was proud, and any closet racists remained silent. On the surface, everything appears ideal.

And yet, ask ten Slovenians if they are a tolerant people, and you will receive five emphatic yeas and five confident nays. This ambivalence is due to both compartmentalization—that is, choosing which particular groups and individuals to tolerate—and the mild-mannered Slovenian ways. Slovenians are delighted to engage with presentable Westerners and nonwhite foreigners. On the other hand, those from the former Yugoslavia are treated with varying degrees of suspicion. In general, the further south their hometown, the less accepted they are. At the very least, Slovenians will blithely and kindly refer to "my Serbian dentist" or "my Dalmatian neighbor" even if he or she has lived in the country for decades. Complaints come more in the form of quiet insinuations that during communism southerners who relocated to Slovenia were pampered and could skip the line when waiting for a state apartment. Slovenians happily acknowledge that Serbians and Bosnians have more *joie de vivre*; they know because they all have Serbian and Bosnian friends.

The Roma, or Gypsies, are regarded as dishonest, untrustworthy, violent, unwilling to assimilate, and—worst of all for Slovenians—lazy. Parents sometimes demand classroom segregation, arguing that the Roma have a disregard for education and should thus be sectioned off into their own classes to avoid slowing down the others. In 2006, Slovenia made headlines after a Slovenian who had been living with a thirty-one-member Roma clan (the Strojan family) injured another local Slovenian in a fight. Residents from and around the village of Ambrus chased away the clan, claiming that they were squatters. The government found accommodation for them elsewhere, thereby turning the fiasco into a rights issue because it appeared to be condoning forceful removal.

THE SLOVENIAN SIN: STICKING OUT

Slovenians do not like to stand out. They have a desire for moderation in everything but food and drink, they avoid risk, and they are nowhere near as temperamental as their southern neighbors. On the whole, the country has a northern, quaintly Austrian feel to it. Those Slovenians who put themselves on display, or speak too loudly or too much, are a reviled species. Bragging is abhorred.

Because they are eager to do a good job, always, Slovenians have an acute fear of failing publicly. Consequently, they are a quiet, even conformist, bunch when in a crowd. They are comfortable with silence, and asking for a volunteer generally results in a silence that may be misunderstood. Slovenians generally mind their own business, and will not pry or press you for information, regardless of how interested they may be; nor will they always rush unbidden to provide aid. This can be mistaken for coldness or Germanic reserve. If you need help, be sure to ask directly—you'll be happily surprised at the immediate change in attitude.

ATTITUDES TOWARD EDUCATION

Slovenian schools are good, but there is nevertheless a puzzling reverence for formal education and paper accreditation. Every one-day educational seminar or course, no matter how trifling, concludes with a certificate of attendance akin to the schoolboy's participation ribbon for the three-legged race. It is not so much the educating as the having been educated, as having acquired some sort of title or proof. Impressive-looking titles also appear where you would not see them in other countries; flying in the face of the Romantic artist-as-genius concept, the label *akademski slikar* (academic painter) graces many a Slovenian artwork, indicating that there is a degree behind the canvas. Whereas hyper-educated Anglophone politicians drop the PhD or MA for fear of appearing elitist, in Slovenia the opposite is true:

individuals are more likely to flaunt their education. This love of titles is a hand-me-down from Habsburg and Belgrade rule that is at obvious loggerheads with the desire to blend in.

Much of the educational excitement revolves around the very demanding *gimnazija*, the academic high school that funnels the best and brightest young Slovenians off to university. Results of the grueling standardized final high school exam known as the *matura* are followed closely, and plenty of TV and radio time is devoted to the results. It is not unheard of for parents to plead, cajole, and haul in the lawyers to help find an extra exam mark or two for their child. In Slovenia, grades are serious stuff.

Forgoing formal education is a no-no. School days exist forever in the Slovenian memory, and sometimes there are whispers that well-known individuals dropped out of university way back when, as if it were a chink in their armor of success. Newspaper reports regularly refer to a celebrity's education, occasionally mentioning what a singer or businessperson wrote about in a BA thesis in her previous life as a student. To the outsider, this can seem like unnecessary adulation of past merits.

STATUS

An old Slovenian joke goes: "What do you do if your cow dies?" "Pray hard that your neighbor's cow will also die." Intended to highlight the

Slovenians' allegedly jealous nature, this joke is also related to status, because people here are acutely aware of their neighbors' material well-being. "Status" is often used as a direct synonym for "money." Accept this and you will more easily understand it when Slovenians speak of a "lack of status" in their job; it simply means they feel they are underpaid, rather than wanting in nonfinancial accolades. They are always aware of the injustice of pay structures and conventions—that is, they are ever watchful of what their coworkers earn. There is a widespread belief that one should automatically be paid for exams passed long ago rather than according to market supply and demand, or even workplace performance.

For a society weaned on socialism, Slovenians are highly class-conscious. They hate the *nouveaux riches*. There is too often a sense that an individual has gained his wealth through luck and trickery rather than hard work. Individuals who regained family property through denationalization after 1991 are regarded as somehow undeserving of this windfall. Most of the ire, however, is aimed at *tajkuni* (tycoons) who became extraordinarily wealthy in the years after independence by—so goes the usual accusation—abusing communist connections established during Yugoslav times. There are several levels and types of politically motivated accusations, just as there are doubtless many levels and shades of truth to the accusations. The dirty business deeds range from the usual book-cooking and tax evasion, through securing absurdly easy loan terms from former party comrades, to continuing as directors of companies after 1991, intentionally running them into the ground, buying them for a pittance, then reviving them to make a fortune.

WORK ETHIC

For Slovenians, laziness constitutes moral turpitude, and they seem genuinely happy sweating away in a field or in the garden. The Slovenian work ethic is impressive; indeed, in ex-Yugoslavia their southern neighbor painted them as task-focused workaholics. There are also slews of Yugoslav jokes that hinge on the Slovenians' dogged work ethic, contrasting them with the more relaxed Bosnians and Macedonians.

There are, however, some differences between Slovenian and American concepts of hard work. Slovenians do not work fourteen-hour days; they tend to pack up and go home at the stroke of 3:00 p.m., and they never used to take work home. They have strict working hours, and they expect to finish their work within those hours (though this is rapidly changing as their standard 7:00 a.m. to 3:00 p.m. working day is fading into the past). The real work is saved for home and Saturdays (see page 99).

chapter **three**

CUSTOMS & TRADITIONS

HOLIDAYS AND CELEBRATIONS

The hardworking Slovenians are also ardent celebrators. In addition to the religious and state holidays, they find plenty of spontaneous reasons to party. Slovenians mark any occasion or event, and there always seems to be a village band trumpeting the newest stretch of road or tunefully christening a town's refurbished marketplace. Village election campaigns are as much about barbecues and pigs on spits as they are about political platforms and speeches, filling the bellies of the political faithful while offering party crashers the proverbial free lunch. You haven't visited Slovenia until you've been to one of these splendid local festivals or parties. Such events are very public and inclusive, so join in when a village celebrates its new bit of sidewalk, or places a commemorative plaque on a building.

Slovenian holidays that fall on a weekend are not carried over to the next working week.

CHRISTMAS

During Yugoslav times, Christmas was just another working day, and families who wanted to celebrate

PUBLIC HOLIDAYS	
Jan. 1, 2	**New Year** *Novo leto*
February 8	**Prešeren Day** *Slovenski kulturni praznik (“Prešernov dan”)*
March/April	**Easter Monday** *Velikonočni poedeljek*
April 27	**Uprising Against Occupation Day** *Dan upora proti okupatorju*
May 1, 2	**May Day Holiday** *Praznik dela*
June 25	**Statehood Day** *Dan državnosti*
August 15	**Assumption Day** *Marijino vnebovzetje*
October 31	**Reformation Day** *Dan reformacije*
November 1	**Day of Commemoration of the Dead** *Dan spomina na mrtve*
December 25	**Christmas Day** *Božič*
December 26	**Day of Independence and Unity** *Dan samostojnosti in enotnosti*

had to do so on their own time. Now it is once again an official holiday and a day off work (actually two, since another, the Day of Independence and Unity, falls on December 26). Christmas remains a private affair, limited mainly to the immediate family. Workplaces will honor the holiday season by having a get-together around Christmas, but to avoid offending the nonreligious it won't be called a Christmas party. Similarly, neighbors or coworkers may present you with a small consumable "New Year's gift," such as chocolate or wine.

Far from the madding crowds and cries of mall-world, many towns erect Christmas markets in temporary wooden huts. Here you'll find an assortment of winter-themed gifts ranging from snuggly slippers and mittens, through hand-painted glass, to plastic kitsch. A Christmas market is a charming place to spend an evening, strolling—mulled wine in hand—through decorated streets and under glittering holiday lights.

The main religious festivities, as well as gift giving, are on December 24 rather than Christmas Day. Early evening is also when the family traditionally decorates the Christmas tree. After that, there is much eating to fortify oneself for the crowded Midnight Mass. The Christmas Eve spread consists of a proper meal, generally ham, topped off by the traditional cake known as *potica* (see page 113). On December 25 the immediate family will meet up again for some more eating. There is no obligatory turkey or goose. Ham is typical, but not essential.

Children are the big winners during the holiday season, as the mixture of religious and less pious traditions keeps the gifts coming through

December. Even before Christmas arrives, increasingly with a gift from Santa Claus, some children receive goodies on December 6. That is the day Miklavž, or St. Nicholas, leaves candies and other small treats for obedient children. In theory, children who have behaved badly are beaten with a stick by Parkelj, Miklavž's hard-hearted alter ego, but no Slovenian child is ever sufficiently wicked to reap this punishment. Unlike other countries, where St. Nicholas is feted in a secular, Halloween-like manner, Miklavž retains a more religious air, and children of nonbelievers don't get to revel in this sugar-fest.

CARNIVAL (PUST)

Carnival, or Pust, precedes Lent, and is a movable feast in all senses. Falling in late February or early March, depending on the date of Easter, Pust is a frolicking bacchanalia enjoyed before believers settle down to the Lenten fast. Though no one knows its exact roots, there is a definite pagan connection to the festival, for it was at this time that pre-Christians rejoiced as the end of winter coaxed the beginning of spring and a fruitful crop.

The key figure of this holiday is the *kurent*, a mythological beast that literally cannot stand still. Originating from near the town of Ptuj, the *kurent* mask and costume is one of the many such traditional items that individual villages bring

out to celebrate Pust. A *kurent* costume approaches a hundred pounds in weight, consists of much sheepskin, a leather mask, massive boots, and enormous bells, and makes a terrible racket as the inhabitant tries to scare winter and demons away. For added effect, a *kurent* carries a wooden club. Formerly only bachelors could don the costume, as it was a time to seek nubile partners, and available males went out on the hunt for girls. Today *kurenti* continue to approach young women with a lustful gleam in the eye. Tradition dictates that girls should return the attention by tying a colorful handkerchief to the already vibrant *kurent* costume.

EASTER

Slovenians follow the Western Church calendar. Note that Good Friday is a working day, and Easter Monday is the day off.

Until quite recently Easter in Slovenia brought about more concentration on faith and ritual than chocolate Easter eggs. Now, as with the Christmas season, there are decorations and bunnies aplenty in the supermarkets.

Traditional markets, meanwhile, do a brisk business in decorative arrangements of branches or twigs, often brightened by thick colored wood shavings. These little bouquetlike creations, known as *butarice* (along with several other region-specific names), are made of everything from olive to hazel to juniper, come in all sizes, and are definitely worth a pre-visit Internet image search. One week before Easter, on Palm Sunday, they are carried to the church to be blessed, then brought back and mounted on a wall to protect the household.

Easter arrives with a bang. Literally. On Holy Saturday the explosions begin as men place chunks of calcium carbide in barrels, sprinkle water over them to produce a dangerous gaseous mixture, and then light a match. The explosions might wake the dead, and definitely spook the living as the hills amplify the thunderous noise. At some point these pyrotechnics were meant to evoke the biblical passage in which Jesus yielded up the ghost, when "the veil in the Temple was rent in twain," and there was a great noise. Nowadays it is just an excuse for big boys to make loud bangs.

The faithful spend part of Saturday in quieter surroundings. Women head with their baskets to church for the blessing of the Easter meal: ham,

colored Easter eggs, bread, horseradish root, and *potica* for dessert. Easter Sunday means plenty of eating and good times spent in the company of the family, and even nonbelievers tend to match their big Sunday meal to the season.

NEW YEAR

For children, the end of the year is when the long-awaited Dedek Mraz, or "Grandfather Frost" comes to town. Invented during socialist times, this figure—who looks like a white-clad Miklavž—arrives to distribute gifts in kindergartens and schools. Slovenian children may be coddled, but they are not often spoiled in material terms, so December is a particularly happy month for them because Miklavž, Santa Claus, and Dedek Mraz may all visit.

The New Year is a more social occasion than Christmas, and December 31 is when the big holiday parties and dancing and cork-popping occur. Slovenians are wild about fireworks, and every village worth its salt will put on a lavish display and accompanying party with a live band.

The festivities are soured only by the hordes of adolescents igniting firecracker after firecracker in the midst of the masses. Come midnight, be prepared to waltz into the dawn as you briefly remember that Slovenia was once ruled from the Strausses' Vienna.

January 1 is a family occasion and another big day of eating. Even among close friends and family, congratulations and best wishes are doled out with great solemnity. A minor warning is in order here: merely calling out a hearty "Happy New Year!" across a room or hallway is a no-no. A verbal New Year's greeting requires an accompanying handshake. As with so much in Slovenia, this seasonal well-wishing is sincere, not just a casual platitude. Approach the other person and offer him or her your hand.

ALL SAINTS' DAY

Because Slovenians' fixation on death wavers between refreshing honesty and downright morbidity, November 1 is arguably the big holiday. In Slovenia, death is ever in view, not hidden away in the Anglo-Saxon style, and the dead are long remembered. Slovenians tend their cemeteries as carefully as they clean their houses. A quick stroll through a village cemetery is worthwhile and, astonishingly, you may see that graves of individuals who died thirty or more years ago are impeccably maintained and adorned with a variety of flowers and a candle or two.

On this day each grave in the cemetery is a miniature botanical garden as the wreaths and flowers pile up. After dark, candle-rich village cemeteries look like tiny cities of light. In keeping with this respect for the dead and refusal to forget, All Saints' Day is perhaps the quintessential Slovenian holiday (the literal translation from the Slovenian is the less religious-sounding "Day of Commemoration of the Dead"). This day off work is far more taxing than a regular eight hours on the job—everyone dresses to the nines and heads to the graveyard to mingle with friends from school who have returned to their home villages to visit the living and the dead. Despite the somber occasion, the main sport is to look one's best and to be seen placing the prettiest arrangement of flowers and candles on the family grave.

OTHER OCCASIONS

Slovenian men observe or forget Valentine's Day in much the same way as their Western brethren. Flowers and other small gifts are the norm; plenty of saccharine pop concerts are scheduled on or around February 14, and this is the busiest week of the year for crooners.

International Women's Day sounds as though it should be a great day of emancipation, marches, and protest against inequality and sexism, but appearances deceive. March 8 basically means that men must buy flowers for their mothers-in-law and other important women in their lives.

St. Martin's Day is an important annual festival celebrated on November 11, the day that *mošt* or new wine is said to turn into proper wine. The world's oldest grape vine is conveniently located in the center of Maribor and it is there that the largest party is held. Thousands gather to dance, indulge, and imbibe, all in the name of fall, Martin, and the latest vintage. The central event is the symbolic baptism of the new wine, so that it may begin its new life as real *vino*.

Thematically linked to and prior to St. Martin's Day is *trgatev*, or grape harvesting. Family and friends are invited to pick the grapes for future vintages. This is no mere abuse of friendship to gain free labor, for it is an honor to be invited to a *trgatev*. Each generation does its part: the young pick the grapes, the older generations guard the vats and press the grapes, and the most able-bodied shuttle back and forth from vineyard to wine cellar with a wicker backpack. Many of the women get busy preparing a feast for when the work is done.

Koline is another festive day of work. Family and friends gather to slaughter a pig and prepare sausages, cutlets, and other meaty supplies for the long winter. No occasion for the faint of heart, this day represents a link to Slovenia's rural roots and is a reminder that the best products are homegrown or homemade. Securing meat from a local farmer is a folk sport in Slovenia.

NATIONAL HOLIDAYS

Slovenians haul out and wave their flags only on state holidays, which they celebrate with minimal pomp but maximal awareness of circumstance. Most Slovenians clearly remember the events that led to independence, and it is for this reason that ceremonies are earnest rather than jovial. There is none of the New World glee surrounding Independence Day in the United States.

Prešeren Day

The national poet, France Prešeren, died on February 8, 1949, which is now "Slovenian Cultural Holiday" or, more popularly, "Prešeren Day." Prešeren, who was unrecognized during his unhappy and love-free earthly existence, is now *the* cultural icon of the young state. One of his poems is now the national anthem, his statue overlooks the main square in Ljubljana, schoolchildren learn and memorize details about his life, and when a biographical film released about ten years ago portrayed the artist as a heavy drinker there were protests. Translations of Prešeren's poetry are widely available, and there is even an English-language CD available, with no less than Simon Callow and Vanessa Redgrave reciting Prešeren's poetry. Those less enamored of verse can enjoy spherical chocolate products comically named in honor of the poet. Both the chocolate and the English on the packaging are sure to bring a smile to your face.

Each February 8 Slovenian culture is on everyone's mind. On this day, one can be sure of three things: a day off work, the bestowing of the various Prešeren Awards, and heated debate about the televised show, which often provides space for acts that are too avant-garde for many viewers' tastes. And yet there is a heartfelt obligation to tune in. What better way of celebrating culture than to critique it?

Day of Uprising Against Occupation

Until 1992 this holiday, which survived the transition from Yugoslavia to independence, was known as the Day of the Liberation Front. April 27 commemorates a crucial turning point in modern Slovenian history: the forming of the resistance movement in 1941. Made up of various groups with various ideologies,

the Liberation Front was led by the outlawed Communist Party. Until then there was minimal resistance against the occupying powers (and it is for this reason that many Slovenians remember late 1941, when bullets began to fly over Slovenian soil, as the beginning of the Second World War). The day is marked by solemn speeches and renewed calls for unity regardless of ideological or political direction.

May Day(s)

Like Labor Day, May Day reminds everybody of the workers' ongoing contribution to the nation's welfare. One can celebrate the spirit of solidarity and all the rest in formal ceremonies, but many Slovenians seize the days (May 2 is also a holiday) to go to the Adriatic coast. May 1 offers a tempting taste of summer. Relaxation is part and parcel of the two-day holiday, and woe to the unwitting professor who announces a test for April 30 or the unschooled foreign businessman who schedules an important meeting—the May holidays are often unofficially stretched to a full week, starting as early as April 27. In this regard, everyone strictly observes the Socialist tradition that gave rise to the modern concept of May Day.

If you drive through villages on May 1, you will see groups of men raising the May tree—in other words, arguing about the best way to make the massive stripped and decorated pine tree pole stand up. This popular tradition harks back to ancient fertility rites and the return of warm weather.

Statehood Day

On June 25, 1991, Slovenia declared independence from Yugoslavia, setting the stage for a short war. Though the Yugoslav troops began to retreat from Slovenian territory already in early July, 1991, and though there was minimal bloodshed in Slovenia, this was also the day when the horrific wars in the Balkans began. Each year there is an official ceremony held in Ljubljana at the Republic Square on the evening of June 24.

Reformation Day

Reformation Day is a surprising national holiday for a country culturally and historically dominated by Roman Catholicism. On October 31, 1517, Martin Luther nailed his ninety-five theses to a church door in Wittenberg, ruffling the Pope's feathers and eventually setting off religious wars. Because the Reformation meant so much to the development of Slovenian culture—especially through the writings of Primož Trubar (see page 27)—Slovenians reverently observe this holiday.

Independence and Unity Day

Some countries' Boxing Day is Slovenia's Independence and Unity Day. On December 26, 1990, the results of the December 23 referendum on creating an independent Slovenia became known. To a tantalizingly clear question—"Should Slovenia become an independent and sovereign state?"—93.2 percent answered "Yes." The government made good its promise to respect the voice of the people by declaring independence within six months (hence Statehood Day in late June). Packed as it is within the busy holiday season, Independence and Unity Day is the silent little sister among the official state holidays. Most people are home for the holidays with their immediate families.

HATCHED, MATCHED, AND DISPATCHED

Slovenian birthrates are low, and long gone are the days of massive Catholic families. Names are overtly biblical in derivation, and for generations Jože and Marija (Joseph and Maria) were the standards, while the gospel quartet of Matej, Marko, Luka, and Janez were equally popular. Today, the top female names across the Slovenian population—including young and old—are Marija, Ana, Maja, and Mojca, and the most frequent male names are Franc, Janez, Anton, Ivan, and Jožef. Middle names are uncommon. Indeed, in some areas everyone seems to be named Anton, and the schoolteacher who has failed to memorize the names of students can safely yell out "Maja!" to get a response, since there is one in every room.

Though many lament that young parents now mine American soap operas and *telenovele* for flashy foreign names, statistics disprove this pop culture influence. There have, however, been new naming patterns since 1991. The Germanic-sounding Rajmund and the pan-Slavonic Radoslav and Radivoj have lost ground, but more than a few kindergartens now have at least one young Melany or Etjan (phonetic renderings of "Melanie" and "Étienne") running the halls. The *ur*-Slovenian Alenka still pops up with startling regularity.

Weddings

The civil ceremony takes place in the town hall or other municipal edifice. Here, a city official delivers a heartfelt and serious speech in what is for many just the first half of the wedding process—because of the strict church–state division, and because a priest cannot sign the legal documents, a church wedding means a second ceremony.

Those lucky enough to be invited to both the ceremony and the reception are in for a treat. In villages everyone is invited to the party, but in towns the guest list is more limited. If you are invited to the wedding, be generous with the gift. Though gift registries are coming into vogue, there is no shame in consulting the almost-weds before purchasing a gift. When in doubt, some guests simply put fifty euros, or more, into an envelope.

Food is plentiful, and guests should pace themselves. A menu card is rarely provided, so beware: the first meat platter is just a prelude to an appetizer and the main course is still a few plates away. A Slovenian wedding often contains three meat courses and at least two sweet dishes, sometimes topped off with sausage around midnight. There will be no shortage of alcohol. Champagne or wine toasts follow both the civil and the church wedding, guests are welcomed to the restaurant with a glass of homemade schnapps, and wine flows freely throughout the evening.

Entertainment generally consists of some live music or a DJ used to playing to all generations. Polkas are a given, and guests can also expect a series of games and other pleasant shenanigans punctuating the evening. Also, the bride may be "stolen" by friends of the groom, which means that the non-vigilant maid of honor will have to buy a meal for the abductors at some time in the future. Why? Clearly she has failed to take proper care of the bride, and should be punished for ignoring the main maiden.

The Abraham

At least as important as a wedding among Slovenians is an "Abraham," or fiftieth birthday. The name stems from the biblical passage John 8: 57, in which Jesus is accused of being too big for his breeches because he claims to be older than Abraham ("Thou art not yet fifty years old, and hast thou seen Abraham?"). While all agree that this is a momentous occasion, there are competing views about its meaning. The glass-is-half-full interpretation holds that fifty is still young; the glass-is-half-empty view sees things differently—the party is a harbinger of old age. Regardless of which is correct, a grand feast with many glasses to fill and empty, as well as many contemplative and wise speeches, is the norm.

Funerals

Slovenians look death straight in the eye. Funerals are grand affairs, and secular and religious ceremonies alike can last for several hours. On the day of the funeral, the immediate family and closest friends of the deceased converge at the cemetery early in the morning, later greeting the other black-dressed mourners. It is not uncommon to hear a band playing a Partisan or religious tune, and the funeral procession is as slow and dignified as death deserves. Most bodies are cremated. Unlike widows in some Catholic countries, a Slovenian woman does not wear mourning after the death of her husband.

Extravagant wreaths, rather than donations to charity, are how one shows one's respect. As well, graves overflow with red, plastic-cased candles.

chapter **four**

MAKING FRIENDS

Slovenians do not fool around with friendship. This is why they are surprised at how often and readily English speakers use the word "friend" for someone they would consider an acquaintance. This sounds insincere to Slovenians, since, if you consider everyone a friend, who is then a real friend? Dictionaries tell us that "*prijatelj*" means "friend," but a more accurate rendering would be "very, very good friend." In fact, young people have coined the word "*frend*" or "*frendica*" (the female equivalent) to indicate that a mate is more than just a peer but not yet a bosom buddy.

Having a great many friends is not fathomable to most Slovenians; they are used to perhaps three or four. Everyone else is an acquaintance, and so the word "acquaintance" does not have the distancing meaning it does in English. You can spend many a pleasant hour with an acquaintance and remain amiably on the formal "*vi*" for decades (see below, page 88).

While a friend is by general definition someone you can depend on, the Slovenians are particularly aware of this. A friend is someone who will readily help you out, even if you haven't spoken in years, and will be equally willing to call you when they are in need. Accordingly, Slovenians are reticent about asking even good acquaintances for a favor, and if you do something small for a neighbor you may find them disproportionately grateful.

FRIENDS FOR LIFE

Real friendships in Slovenia are formed in primary school, secondary school, or university, and last a lifetime. However, though these old friends are the nearest and dearest ones, it does not mean that there are daily or weekly telephone calls to catch up on the latest news and gossip, or that they will drop in unannounced. It does not mean that contact will continue uninterrupted through the months and years, but conversation will resume easily even after long breaks.

Neighbors remain acquaintances for life and there is no social imperative to become pals just because you happen to live next to each other. Though generally cordial, neighborly relations are somewhat aloof. You can live for years without ever seeing the inside of a neighbor's house or apartment. Slovenians do not pop in to borrow the proverbial cup of sugar from a neighbor in the apartment building (it's not a social transgression, it's just not usual); on the other hand, a neighbor may drop off some baking or freshly picked produce, and around harvest time *sosedi* (neighbors) enthusiastically exchange bags of apples or grapes. Elderly ladies are universally concerned about men's ability to feed themselves, and if word gets out that madam has gone away for a few days, the monsieur may find himself eating like an exiled king. Lastly, because the Slovenian gossip mill grinds flawlessly, your neighbors will know all about you, even if they leave you in peace.

MEETING PEOPLE

Though you as a foreigner will encounter friendliness everywhere you go in Slovenia, it is very difficult to make friends. In towns and cities, some effort is required on your part to meet people. The general assumption is that if you are alone, you want to be left alone, and the Slovenians don't get too personal too fast. In other words, there is no mad dash to wine and dine the newcomer.

Generally, you must take the initiative if you want to establish a circle of acquaintances: ask people out for coffee, ask if you can join the local lads for pickup soccer or basketball, and join the village camera club or folk dance group if it appeals to you. Once you meet one or two people, things change quickly and soon enough the acceptance and invitations will come—"Any buddy of Marko's is a buddy of mine!"

Some visitors have noticed a peculiar manifestation of Slovenian modesty: people who speak admirable English often clam up when in a group. There is widespread fear among Slovenians that their English is somehow inadequate—though it will of course be miles ahead of your Slovenian—and they want to avoid embarrassing themselves by letting slip a flawed accent or shoddy grammar in front of their peers. This often dovetails with a legitimate pride in protecting Slovenian, but the result can be uncomfortable for visitors. You may find three hours of Slovenian dinner conversation framed by a curt "Hello!" and a brief "Good-bye!"

CONVERSATION

Slovenians are more reserved than their neighbors from ex-Yugoslavia, from Italy to the west and even the Austrians, and they don't leap into conversation with strangers on trains or buses or in cafés. You can observe this in the coffeehouses, where there is little group chattiness or banter among regulars who don't know each other. You are unlikely to make acquaintances in a café.

People in trains are not unfriendly, just silent and not given to chatting. Slovenians generally find small talk superficial. If something out of the ordinary happens—such as the announcement of a lengthy delay or something else to complain about—conversation begins smoothly and naturally, as if everyone were just waiting for an icebreaker.

Don't be shy about starting a conversation, though, since a Slovenian will generally be happy to continue it. (A note for those learning Slovenian: they tend to fall silent when they hear someone struggling with their language. Grandmothers, the exception to the rule, are excellent language teachers.) Even if your neighbors wonder what you are doing in Slovenia, or how you came to live here or visit, they will restrain themselves from asking. Many are genuinely interested, though, and once the conversational doors are open, the questions may come quickly.

The art of Slovenian conversation is difficult to master. While people are seldom bigoted or even boisterous, their talk is more direct and less irony-filled than you may be used to. Your deadpan humor will not bring down the house. If someone disagrees with you, don't expect kid gloves as they inform you of the "truth" of a matter. And yet this truth is delivered without badgering, browbeating, or a fight-to-the-death desire to convince you of your ignorance. When it comes to taboo topics (see below), what Slovenians see as the truth is nothing to get emotional about.

There is little tradition of conversational turn taking and communal development of a line of thought. In plain English: Slovenians are prone to interrupting. Interruptions are not uncommon and are not always viewed as rude. Don't be insulted if someone cuts you off after he thinks he's understood your point or predicted your question.

On the whole, though, Slovenians follow the same unspoken rules in conversation as in the West. They are refreshingly direct and unlikely to skate around contentious issues. They save time by telling it like it is. Finally, remember that you'll be talking to individuals rather than types.

HUMOR

Slovenian humor is straightforward, often bawdy, and devoid of political correctness. Newspapers regularly print sexist jokes about witless blondes and housewives who behave improperly, and sometimes they even print racist jokes. The main targets, however, are Slovenia's "southern brothers"—that is, Macedonians and Bosnians, who are portrayed as lazy and dim-witted. Jokes about the various regions within Slovenia are also common, with the allegedly tightfisted people from Gorenjska being the butt of those jokes.

Gentle teasing is foreign to many Slovenians, who tend to opt for fawning admiration or caustic sarcasm. Self-deprecation, too, is unknown, and there is no middle ground between conceitedness and extreme self-belittlement. Slovenians don't generally trouble themselves with understatement and irony. A joke, after all, is a joke: why beat around the bush with coy indirectness?

TABOO TOPICS

Slovenian taboo topics can surprise the visitor because on the surface there appear to be none. Slovenians talk more openly of sex and other intimacies than Anglo-Saxon cultures do; while money is a constant topic, Slovenians do not speak of personal finances, and they modestly play down new acquisitions such as a car.

The biggest taboo topic is twentieth-century history, more specifically, the Second World War and its aftermath in Tito's Yugoslavia. In this regard, outsiders are in an advantageous position. While it is hardly a topic for a first date, Slovenians are often willing to open up and inform foreigners about the history of their country—as long as you don't attempt to impose your own views of the history of their country, you're fine. Since everyone has a personal story about lining up for sugar, smuggling Western goods across the border, or murder, it is rewarding to listen and receive.

Swearing

Slovenians can swear like sailors, and conversations among men frequently abound with references to sexual acts involving mothers and/or some sort of religious blasphemy. Swearwords one would expect to hear only in the direst circumstances permeate harmless chatter and pleasant conversations. Curiously, Slovenians claim that they don't have any swearwords of their own, that these words are imports from Italian, Croatian, or Serbian, languages with a proper arsenal of four-letter-words. Literal translations into English inevitably add degrees of crudeness, since in context many of these dire-sounding expressions have the softness of "darn" or "damn." If a Westerner says one of these naughty words, the word suddenly sounds harsh to Slovenians.

INVITATIONS

Slovenians mean it when they say you should visit them some day, and there is no such thing as a false invitation, even if it comes at the last minute. If the invitation is for around midday, expect a full meal. If you are invited in the evening or late afternoon, it is likely to be more casual: coffee and cake or a *delikatesa* plate of cheese and cold cuts. For group gatherings, a written reply is polite. A tour of the house is not a given, though by no means forbidden; the doors to individual rooms are closed to save energy.

Slovenians are forever going out for coffee, and are much less prone to "doing lunch"—The coffee-to-lunch meeting ratio is probably ten to one. Lunch invitations tend to be reserved for special occasions, like birthdays or graduations, and are usually for larger groups. It is the custom for the one who does the inviting to pay for everything. Thus, if you invite someone for a coffee or a meal, it is assumed that you will cover the cost. Though you may not remember who actually suggested coffee, your companion will.

You may face adamant demands that he or she pay the bill. Things work out evenly over time, as it is understood that your turn to pay is next.

Office parties are limited to the person employed at the firm; no husbands, wives, or partners are expected (bear this in mind whenever you receive an invitation. If you do plan to bring your other half, mention it ahead of time, or at least ask first).

Gifts

Whenever you are invited to someone's house, bring a small gift. The most obvious choices are wine, chocolate, and flowers or, ideally, something you've baked or distilled yourself. These little items need not be expensive, but don't scavenge a packet of stale cookies from the supermarket discount bin; your hosts will notice the cheapness of the gift and the thought. Flowers have a codified tradition, so unless romancing is your aim, hold off on red roses. Unless you're visiting the dead, hold off on chrysanthemums. Also, do not try to woo somebody with an even number of flowers: odd numbers are for the living.

MANNERS

The comedian George Carlin once said, "There's nothing to do in an elevator, except not talk to the other person." Here there is a pleasant surprise in Slovenia: the same people who do not rush into conversation with strangers always say "Hello" and "Good-bye" when entering and leaving an elevator. Similarly, it is polite to say "*Dober dan*" ("Hello") and "*Nasvidenje*" ("Good-bye") or the less formal but more pronounceable "*Adijo*" when entering and leaving a shop or a restaurant (see page 155).

Slovenian has two ways of saying "you" in the singular, which is a simple fact that English speakers love to complicate. It is courteous and respectful to use the formal "*vi*" with adults; "*ti*" is used when addressing family members, children, and close friends (as well as among the under-thirty crowd at parties, soccer matches, and the like). Always wait for the older person to say, "You can say *ti* to me," and you won't offend anyone.

Good table manners will serve you well in Slovenia. There are, however, a few minor things to watch out for: when invited to someone's house, have a pretty good excuse for refusing a drink, look people directly and warmly in the eye when clinking glasses, and be prepared to eat directly from a communal salad bowl—that is, to jab your fork into the same bowl as everyone else.

When greeting people, handshakes are more common than kisses on the cheek. Further confusing the kiss question is regional variation:

in some areas, such as near the Italian border, it is usual. In others, not. Before you pucker up, see what the other person does. There's no harm in asking whether to give two, three, or zero pecks on the cheeks.

LINE-UP?

Slovenians do not line up in an orderly fashion, and some visitors find this rude. Arriving at the bank or the post office half an hour before the doors open is no guarantee of a pole position. Once the doors open, it's every man for himself, and the last shall indeed sometimes be first. If three tellers or cashiers are open for business, there are usually three lines rather than a single long one ushering customers to the next available agent. This means that picking the right line is a crucial act of prophecy. If a fourth position opens, join the rush. Be aware that retirees have the sharpest elbows.

Slovenians seem to butt in not to provoke others or to save time but for the sake of it. It is not impossible to see the same person who bolted ahead of you search with agonizing slowness for his wallet before chatting up the teller or cashier for a few minutes. Though at some level people realize what they are doing, it is all dished out and accepted with a cool nonchalance and lack of aggression. This is, after all, the most minor of life's inconveniences.

DATING

Slovenians have a down-to-earth concept of love and romance. Star-crossed lovers are fine and dandy for films, but few Slovenians expect to pick up a dream boy or girl in a café. Most Slovenians meet their mates through school or other group environments. Though things are changing—and Slovenians also now exploit the Internet when looking for partners—in villages many couples have been together since time out of mind, or at least since high school or university.

Dinner and a movie is not the standard first date here, and there are few rules or guidelines for the first meeting (though generally the man is expected to pay as well as make the first move). On the one hand, this leads to more natural matchmaking, since acquaintances progress to boyfriend and girlfriend without much ado; on the other, the lack of clear signals can mean that a friendly coffee will be understood as just that, and nothing more.

Westerners will find dating quite straightforward, because relationships in Slovenia operate according to the same rules as in English-speaking countries. There are, however, conflicting accounts of the speed at which the Slovenian dating game progresses:

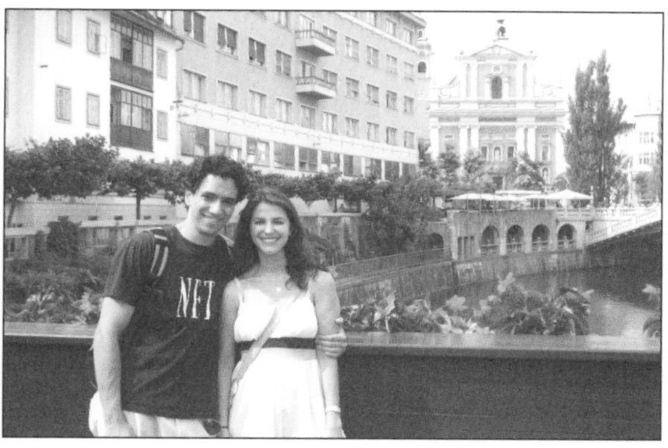

though many people claim that Slovenians are quick to jump into the sack and make things serious, just as many claim that progress is glacial and stamina is required. Foreigners with money will be happy or chastened to learn that there are no gold diggers hoping to land a rich Westerner. There are no online catalogs offering Slovenian mail order brides.

chapter **five**

THE SLOVENIANS AT HOME

FAMILY LIFE

While the family unit is important everywhere, in Slovenia it is integral to people's lives. Even in those rare families that are not close, the parents will know all the goings-on in the lives of their offspring. These matters are discussed openly and frankly, whether it's a problem with the schoolyard bully at primary school, or financial difficulties with grown-up children. In Slovenia, two generations of adults commonly live under one roof, regardless of whether the adult children can afford to move out. This is a throwback to the days of a less prosperous Slovenia and larger families.

Like the rest of the Western world, Slovenians now have small families, and birthrates are low. In recent years, the divorce rate has ranged from about 30 to 35 percent—somewhat lower than the European Union average. However, many do not get married in the first place; the taxman smiles on single parents, and there is therefore an economic incentive to stay single in legal and bureaucratic terms.

Slovenian parents are definitely more hands-on than their Anglophone counterparts. They are very protective, but also critical of their children. Any trip to a local playground confirms this: you will hear parents shouting out a stream of instructions and admonitions to the young ones, even if little Janez does not appear to be in any danger and even if little Maja has done nothing visibly wrong. Often one has the impression

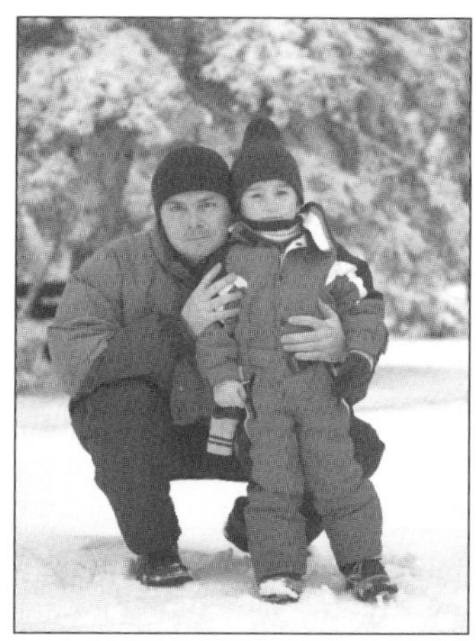

that parents are making a show of being actively vigilant parents through this playground kibitzing.

Women do the bulk of the housework, regardless of whether they are in fact the sole breadwinner, and men generally shy away from doing the dishes or cooking. Anything to do with tools or household machinery is, however, the man's job: mowing the lawn, shoveling snow, and so on. In the garden there is often gender equality (see below), as men and women will shovel and weed side-by-side.

SCHOOLDAYS

From cradle to diploma, young people can expect high-quality public education. Any high school graduate will have acquired solid skills in mathematics and reading, along with foreign language skills that are the envy of the English-speaking world. The downsides to the Slovenian educational system are a lingering Central European fascination with learning by heart, a corresponding lack of independent thinking in the classroom, and underdeveloped analytical skills.

Slovenians often speak of the need for "socialization," which in plain English means that they believe children should be sent to preschool as soon as possible in order to mingle with other kids. Preschool is partially subsidized and parents pay according to their income level.

Regular school begins at age six, when well over 90 percent of children enter the public system. The formerly rigid Slovenian education system, where the teacher was the boss and silence was expected of pupils, has eased up considerably in recent years as a result of a recent education reform that focused more on group work and flexibility in primary school.

However, once pupils hit high school at age fifteen, things become as structured as they were in the pre-reform days. There are two basic options: the university-oriented *gimnazija* (see page 56), and a range of vocational schools for those going in for such occupations as gardening, farming, hairdressing, or tourism and hospitality. Unfortunately, too many parents see the *gimnazija* as the best choice for their child, and there is a mad push to get children into that type of school.

School is a family affair in Slovenia. Parents are intensely involved in their children's schooling, not least because it is not possible to drift casually through the rigorous Slovenian education system without studying. Helping one's child with homework assignments is expected, extra private tutoring is *de rigueur* (even if done on the sly to keep the neighbors from gossiping), and only the crafty Slovenian pupil can hide assignments and grades from mommy and daddy. Also, parents are keen to approach teachers to plead for better grades or discuss other matters involving the child's scholastic and general education.

In addition to one-on-one consultations with parents, teachers have regular meetings for the parents of the entire class. Here the class teacher reports on the curriculum and upcoming events and gives a state-of-the-unit address—noting how many in the class are failing math or English, whether there are problems with discipline, and so on. It is as if the class were a football squad.

Come the teenage years, parents tend to give their children a fair amount of freedom. Curfews and other limitations are generally far less of an issue than in the Anglophone world, and even attitudes regarding alcohol, sex, and travel might make the American teenager envious. This is best evinced by the bacchanalian "graduation trips" that mark the start of the final year of high school, where classes of students take off for raunchy fun in the sun at the beach in Greece, Spain, Croatia, or a similar tourist destination. The visitor to Slovenia need only stroll through a local park on a Friday afternoon to see groups of underage teenyboppers drinking themselves silly in broad daylight. Police turn a blind eye to this, and parents appear to take this drunkenness in stride.

AFTER HIGH SCHOOL

Until 2003 young men had to spend several months in the army. Today any young person who has passed the state *matura* exam can head straight to college or university. There are three public universities (in Ljubljana, Maribor, and Koper), one private university (in Nova Gorica), and over twenty private colleges. These institutions vary in reputation and quality, and the unreliable rule of thumb among Slovenians is the older, the better. Because formal education is so highly esteemed, there is a strong social push to get a degree.

University is very much like high school in certain ways: students spend up to thirty hours a week in the classroom or lecture hall, and are expected to learn many things by rote. Other curiosities include rather fluid deadlines for term assignments, and the possibility of re-sitting some exams up to five times. If universities in the English speaking world teach deadlines, Slovenian universities encourage handing in exemplary work, however long it may take. Despite these differences—and despite the relaxed attitude to plagiarism and cheating—standards are high, and being accepted to university is no guarantee of graduating. The Bologna system, which aims to standardize universities throughout Europe, is slowly being implemented.

HOUSE AND HOME

Most Slovenians (approximately 60 percent) live in houses, rather than apartments. These houses differ in style as you travel toward the coast, as the Venetian architectural influence in older villages becomes apparent. Property prices are extremely high in both relative and absolute terms: the average price of land is higher than in Germany, where people earn much more money. However, away from hyper-expensive Ljubljana, rental rates are comparatively low. This is because Slovenians consider it a waste of money to pay for something you do not own.

Apartment Living

Slovenian apartment buildings are generally well maintained and clean, and there is little of the grimness one expects from communist-era relics. Visitors will not find Stalinist-style blocks. Even in those buildings with peeling paint, broken mailboxes, and a graffiti-daubed elevator, the individual apartments will be prim and proper. In other words, once you cross the threshold, you've moved into a world of order. Slovenians take good care of what they own. They claim that buildings in which the residents own the individual units are better maintained than those in which the majority rent—but to all appearances it is the size of the building rather than the percentage of owned units that determines its condition: the larger the block, the less well kept it is.

New property laws dictate that what used to be cooperatives must be switched to condominiums. There is often a mixture of renters and home owners in apartment buildings. During Yugoslav times it was possible for some individuals to purchase an apartment through their employer, but since apartments were guaranteed for life at nominal rental rates, there was little impetus to buy. Indeed, even today there is a sense among many that the place they have been renting for ages was "owed to them"—that is, the true owner is the one who uses the property, not the one with the deed. After independence in 1991 renters had the chance to purchase their apartments at rock-bottom prices, yet many passed up the investment opportunity.

Houses

The Slovenian dream is to have a house of one's own. Slovenians prefer made-to-order homes, and many companies construct prefabricated houses out of high-quality wood or plastic composite materials that allow for more flexibility of design and sturdiness. Colorful façades are all the rage.

The new housing developments springing up within driving distance of larger towns are akin to North American subdivisions, albeit not as large and monotonous—they are smaller, the houses are not all exactly the same, and more space is devoted to the all-important garden. The trend, however, is toward smaller lots so that cookie-cutter–style houses can be crammed into settlements to maximize profits.

Slovenians stay in the nest longer than one might expect, and many do not go through rental years, staying at home saving their money until they can move into a place they've purchased outright. Some, in fact, never move. At the very least, people will return to the spacious ancestral home every chance they get. Ljubljana and Maribor can be eerily quiet on a Sunday afternoon, and even students make a weekly exodus back to their hometowns.

Slovenians clean with demonic fervor, and much of their well-earned reputation for hard work is channeled into pushing a broom in the kitchen or dusting an already dust-free shelf. In winter, many shovel snow not just to clear a path but to lay bare every square inch of asphalt below the white stuff.

. . . and Gardens

Drive through a small village any time between April and September and you will see rows of avid gardeners tending their patches of earthly paradise. Gardens are devoted to both flowers and food, and the time invested in them pays off in financial terms as well as in stress reduction. There is a particular obsession with potatoes.

Apartment dwellers without a garden may have access to a garden plot. One sees many of these plots, which from afar look like shantytowns, squashed into the most unlikely nooks and crannies of urban space. Waste not, want not, is the motto here.

THE DAILY ROUND

Slovenians wake up at the crack of dawn. then grab a slice of bread and some coffee, in order to get to work for 7:00 or 8:00 a.m in the morning, if not earlier. Nursery schools are ready to accept children at 5:30, many grocery stores are open for business by 7:00, and some clothing shops are ready to sell you a pair of jeans or flip-flops at 8:00. Most shops close at 7:00 p.m. Postmen regularly deliver packages at 7:00 in the morning, and if you have work being done on your house, the roofer or plumber may ring your doorbell at a similarly ungodly hour.

Slovenians break for *malica*, a light meal, around 10:00 a.m., but they eat their main meal after work. Those working a typical schedule finish by mid-afternoon, pick up the little ones from nursery school, and hurry home to eat the all-important *kosilo* by 3:30 or 4:00 p.m. The *kosilo*, or lunch, the main family meal, has iconic status, and on Sunday the extended family will come together at midday for a massive meal that begins with soup, usually includes a great deal of meat and potatoes, and concludes with home-baked dessert. Because lunch is so large, Slovenians have only a light snack, such as a sandwich, around 7:00 p.m.

SHOPPING

Whereas even ten years ago many Slovenians shopped for food every day, now they tend to stock up for the week at supermarkets. In some towns there are four or five domestic and foreign chain stores within a fifteen-minute walk. Since many people are willing to drive a few miles to a well-stocked, well-lit modern supermarket, village shops, increasingly, are closing.

Despite this liking for big supermarkets, Slovenians are keenly aware of quality, and many prefer to purchase fruits and vegetables from individual sellers at the street markets. Linked to this is the recent new appearance of the *mlekomat* (milk-o-mat), a milk-dispensing machine, in urban centers. It is amusing to see a fancy car pull up to one of these shacklike structures and a dressed businesswoman get out, empty bottle in hand, for her supply of locally produced fresh milk. That some of these machines pipe out catchy folk tunes only adds to the charm.

This focus on the local is not so much a new trend as a reflection of changing times—in the past it was a given that the vegetables had not traveled far and that the meat counter was stocked with Slovenian goods. Now there are a few low-key campaigns to get people to "shop Slovenian." Many do this, and buy meat, fruits, and vegetables from local farmers. In fact, farmers go from door to door in towns and cities to offer large quantities of potatoes and other produce.

EMPLOYMENT

Slovenian employment practices are tightly linked to an individual's education. A young Slovenian trains for a job, whether this means attending a vocational school for hairdressers or gardeners or studying for a university degree, and then gets a job precisely according to this training. In line with this rigidity is the reluctance to accept foreign degrees, which have to be legally recognized or "nostrified" (a word at home only in the former Habsburg empire).

For the most part, Slovenians prefer to live and work in the area in which they were born. If job opportunities lure them to the capital, they try to escape back to the hometown as often as possible.

For this reason one sees a long line of cars streaming back to Ljubljana every Sunday after a weekend with the parents or former schoolmates.

Employers are required to pay employees' commuting costs—a system that would become cripplingly expensive if every worker had a North American–style commute. Workers also receive a small daily food allowance in their paychecks. About twenty days' paid vacation per year is the norm. Maternity leave is ten months, can be taken by either parent, and job security and position are guaranteed when they return to the workplace.

Slippers

One thing that Slovenians notice about British and American sitcoms is that guests do not remove their shoes in the house. Many are convinced that all Anglophones go tramping through households with muddy-footed abandon. This means that your host may well mumble a halfhearted "leave your shoes on." She is just trying to make you feel at home. Please take your shoes off!

Every household has enough slippers at the ready to shoe a surprise wedding or bar mitzvah, and they expect them to be put to use. Slovenians are often very concerned that cold feet inevitably lead to illness. If you refuse slippers in September and catch a cold in January, the host will know what happened. Don't say you weren't warned.

chapter **six**

TIME OUT

Slovenians value their leisure time, and have a fair amount of it. Work begins painfully early in the day, but this also means that people can get home from work by mid-afternoon and thus have plenty of spare time each day. Also, because many Slovenians work within comfortable distance of their homes, less time is spent in lengthy commuting.

Whether Slovenians spend their free time in the garden, mountain biking over single track paths, or making death-defying Alpine ascents up a clear rock face, nature is the key word. They are fond of the outdoors, any outdoors, and spend many summer hours with family and close friends, drinking coffee and wine under the apple tree or hiking up a hill with them.

VACATIONS

Slovenian law is generous when it comes to holidays: as we have seen, each worker is entitled to twenty days off. Most people will take a block of two weeks in the summer, and then pick and choose individual days throughout the

year. Employers are flexible about the timing of vacations. This is because Slovenians see time off as an integral part of the work year—a time to recharge the batteries in order to ensure quality future work.

More than two-thirds of Slovenians travel somewhere for their holidays—traditionally to the Slovenian or Croatian coast in summer—and the pace of life slows down considerably in July, with business grinding to a near halt in August.

SPORTS

The Slovenian landscape encourages various ways of getting one's thrills from nature, and there are superb opportunities for activities such as paragliding or hang gliding from the foothills of the Julian Alps, white-water rafting in the Soča or Kolpa rivers, and rock climbing just about everywhere.

In terms of competition, Slovenia has had the most success in individual sports (traditionally skiing, and more recently swimming and boxing); the country has also done well in European handball and soccer. In 2002 and 2010, the national soccer team qualified for the World Cup—no small achievement for a country with a population of just over two million.

Individual Slovenians have also excelled at extreme sports, including some truly bizarre athletic undertakings. The late Jure Robič won the grueling Race Across America cycling derby five times, and Davo Karničar has skied down the highest mountains of each of the seven continents, including Everest. But for sheer wackiness, color, and character, Martin Strel is the champion. This hard-drinking, hard-swimming environmentalist has made a life of swimming the lengths of rivers in Slovenia and around the world—most famously, the Amazon (a feat documented in the Sundance Film Festival hit *Big River Man*).

Over the past decade, people have become more health conscious. Colorfully clad cyclists take over secondary roads as soon as there's a bit of sun, whatever the season, and more and more people have taken up jogging. Golf is becoming increasingly popular, though it is still reserved for the wealthy and would-be wealthy—even more so than yachting on the Adriatic coast.

Hiking and skiing are the two main participatory sports.

Hiking/Trekking

There is a long and healthy tradition of hiking and mountain climbing, and it is said that one is not a true Slovenian until one has climbed Mount Triglav. Slovenians head for the hills, either individually or in groups, in any weather. The entire country is crisscrossed by well-marked trails, there are paths to match any fitness level, and each village has its own little hiking club. Check for posters around villages indicating when the next group hike will be. Everyone is welcome.

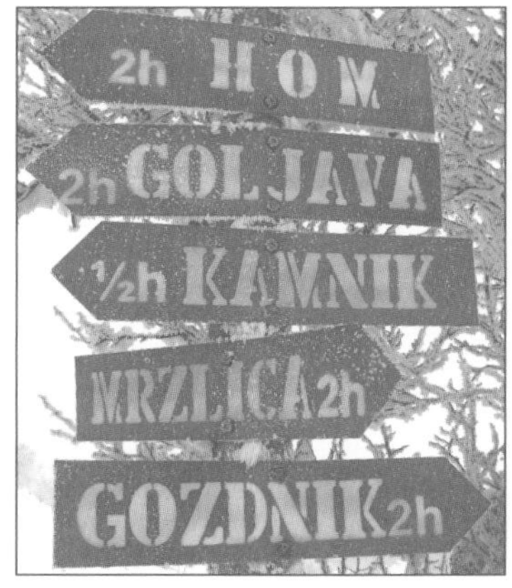

A trip to the hills guarantees running into all types: fanatics who sprint up in the latest and greatest gear, families with little kids perched on their shoulders, and portly individuals who don't look at all sporty. True social equality exists in the hills: everybody chats, there are plenty of smiles, and hiking is without a doubt the best way to meet people. There's even a saying claiming there's no such thing as sin in the mountains.

When hiking, the person going up should be the first to greet. After all, the one descending has already made it to the top, and is thus deserving of a respectful "*Dober dan!*" Also, when you enter the hilltop hut, be sure to belt out a hearty greeting to any fellow mountaineers already there.

Skiing

Skiing goes back at least three hundred years in this part of the world, and because most Slovenians can ski it has retained the air of a folk sport. There are over twenty Alpine ski centers, and it's never

more than an hour to the next ski lift. Skiing in Slovenia, however, is not a bargain, and lift tickets cost approximately the same as in neighboring Austria and Italy. Despite massive investment in new and faster lifts, long lines remain a problem on the slopes.

CULTURAL ACTIVITIES

Orienting oneself in Slovenian culture is a speedy and rewarding process. After visiting just a few art galleries, one can quickly spot the distinctive styles of leading Slovenian artists such as Rihard Jakopič. The number one Slovenian architect by far is Jože Plečnik (1872–1957), an artist of genius who was able to use most of Ljubljana as his three-dimensional canvas. The famous Three Bridges in Ljubljana, the distinctive National and University Library (which looks as if it was designed to be climbed), and many redesigned churches are among his main achievements.

When it comes to culture, however, language is the basis of Slovenian art. The Slovenian book publishing industry is active—to the extent that some people joke that Slovenians write more books than they actually read. Some Slovenian writers say in earnest that they are "victimized from birth" because their language is spoken by so few people. That said, writers' associations have done a splendid job of getting Slovenian works translated into English. Among contemporary writers, the novelists Drago Jančar and Boris Pahor, and the poet Tomaž Šalamun have been capably translated. The somber novels, stories, and sketches of Ivan Cankar (1876–1918) have also been widely translated.

Theater

Each year slightly more than half of the population attends at least one theater production. With nine professional theaters in Slovenia, including some in smallish towns, like Nova Gorica, Celje, and Kranj, culture vultures are spoiled for choice. There are also dozens of other

theaters, offering everything from the familiar to the peculiar—from domestic and mainstream classics played by professionals, to amateur productions in villages, to puppet productions for young and old, from classical ballet to avant-garde dance. There are also two professional opera houses, one in Maribor and one in Ljubljana.

Music

Music is another specialty, and if you're in the mood for a live show—be it Slovenian rap, heavy metal, chansons, jazz, or old-time rock 'n' roll—you will find something in any town.

In terms of traditional music, Slovenia is strongest in two areas: choral music and polka. The choral tradition is impressive, and this is one area of music in which Slovenian composers have done themselves proud. Polka is unavoidable in the best and worst senses (see Buses, page 122), but regardless of your musical taste there's nothing like a tune by Slavko Avsenik to add atmosphere and zest to a party.

Ljubljana is home to two fine orchestras—the Slovenian Philharmonic, whose roots stretch to 1701, and the RTV Slovenia Symphony Orchestra. The Maribor Symphony Orchestra also serves up quality performances of classical music at attractive prices. For twenty euros you are guaranteed a good seat in any Slovenian venue. This is a particularly attractive deal when leading world soloists fly in to play with the house

orchestra, because ticket prices remain the same as for the regular subscription series.

CUISINE

Slovenian cuisine is unpretentious, hearty, and varied, which reflects both the country's rural roots and its geographical position. Proper meals are planned around meat, primarily pork and beef, and not long ago Slovenia was a nightmare land for vegetarians.

Slovenians never used to buy prepared meals, and only recently have supermarkets begun to offer any variety of meals-in-a-bag. When guests come to visit, no respectable Slovenian would dream of offering any dish not made from scratch.

Typical Slovenian foods near the Italian border are *pršut* (prosciutto) and polenta; in Styria and elsewhere near the Austrian border, there is plenty of sausage, pork, and sauerkraut on the menu, while *golaž* (goulash) obviously hails from Hungary. More recently, Slovenia has embraced Serbian and Macedonian culinary traditions, and grilled meat and vegetables are all the rage when the barbecue season arrives.

Over the centuries, Slovenians have learned to do remarkable things with simple ingredients, and the side dishes polenta and *žganci* (a thick type of porridge commonly made with buckwheat or maize) each come in many forms. The local supermarket's bakery section exemplifies this variety in simplicity, as there you can choose from over a dozen types of freshly baked bread.

Just Desserts

Slovenians are extremely proud of *gibanica* and *potica*, two indigenous sweets with untranslatable names. One could describe the first merely as a layer cake, but that wouldn't do justice to this heavy, all-in-one dessert smorgasbord. *Gibanica* contains any combination of poppy seeds, walnuts, *skuta* (a creamy curd cheese, not cottage cheese as many a dictionary claims), and apples, and is usually served warm with a light dusting of sugary icing on top to keep the calorie count up. *Potica* is its quieter, less

decadent little sister. If *gibanica* feels like a meal in itself, *potica* feels like a dieter's light reward after a week of vegetables. Made from a single sheet of pastry, which is then filled with crushed walnuts and rolled, *potica* takes forever to bake and exists in myriad varieties. Every village and valley has its own version (which, of course, is the one true version).

EATING OUT

Until recently, visitors noticed a peculiarity in Slovenia's culinary landscape: each town, regardless of size, was surrounded by restaurants serving indistinguishable varieties of the same tasty but heavy fare. Locals would drive visitors several miles to a "special" place to sup on the set menu consisting of beef broth or mushroom soup, a meat-based main course (usually pork), served with potatoes or dumplings, and vinegary salad. Only a true connoisseur—that is, a Slovenian!—could tell the difference between this menu and that offered nearer to home.

There are now many international culinary options available, including Tex Mex, Japanese, and Chinese. In fact, because Slovenians like to drive to their favorite restaurant, and because many restaurants are located outside towns and cities, it can be difficult to find a traditional Slovenian meal in tourist areas. In towns and cities fine pizzerias with proper wood-burning ovens are ubiquitous.

TIPPING
Slovenians generally do not tip in the American sense, and there is no tradition of leaving coins on the table. The same holds true for taxis and other small services. If a delivery man delivers a heavy package to your door, he is unlikely to refuse a tip, but neither will he expect it. More common than tipping is simply rounding up the bill—if your meal comes to twenty-eight euros, you can say “Thirty” to the waitress; if a coffee is ninety cents, just round up to a euro. You are unlikely to see waiting staff fishing for tips. In fact, waiters at cafés prefer the exact money. Far worse than leaving no tip is to pay for a coffee or a *krof* (donut) with a large bill.

Drinks and Drinking
One does not go thirsty in Slovenia. There are plenty of fine wines available, from light Rieslings like Renski and Laški *rizling*, to the earthy red wine known as *teran*, to the sour, blended *cviček*, which is good fuel for manual labor. As long as you spend more than four euros per bottle, it’s hard to go wrong. At restaurants, the house wine is always drinkable. Beer is also popular, and the two main breweries, Laško (from, yes, Laško) and Union

(from Ljubljana), are in fierce competition for the hearts and taste buds of consumers. Laško is a classic lager, while Union is somewhat sweet.

In addition to beer and wine, there is an array of liqueurs and liquor, of which the plum brandy *slivovec*, with its alcohol content of up to 70 percent, is the most famous and deadly. Slovenians swear by its medicinal qualities, using it to patch over open wounds and cure colds. If plum brandy is not to your taste, you can find alcohol distilled from pears, walnuts, apples, grapes, or herbs. These spirits grow like mushrooms in Slovenian pantries, so look each person in the eye and say "*Na zdravje*!"

Nonalcoholic drinks can also be found. The town of Radenci has been bottling its mineral water for generations, and the Radenska brand was consumed at both the Viennese court and the Vatican. Donat brand mineral water, meanwhile, is known as a remedy for constipation, and is marketed accordingly (one of its ads cleverly included a shapely bum and zipper underwear, to the puzzlement of many a visitor).

On top of homemade schnapps, many Slovenian households produce syrups and juices out of domestic and wild fruits.

BANKS AND PAYING

Slovenian banks open later than shops—generally from 8:30 a.m. to 4:00 p.m. Some small banks close for lunch at midday. Banking services, including levels of friendliness, have improved immensely in recent years. Grumpy and rude tellers are, if not extinct, certainly on the way out. The variety of services available now matches those of English-speaking countries. Banking practices are rather continental—that is, sometimes bewildering when compared to American and British customs. A case in point: when you mention checks, most Slovenians will think of something like travelers' checks rather than a standard payment method. This is because they pay their bills via account-to-account transfer (with a form called a *položnica*).

Within Slovenia and within the Eurozone, electronic bank transfers are convenient. When transferring funds between Slovenia and non-EU countries, however, the process can take weeks and incur exorbitant fees. Automatic tellers are everywhere, and online banking is widespread.

Slovenians often pay with plastic, mainly with debit cards (perhaps because, when you pay with cash, cashiers are fanatical about extracting the exact money from you). Credit card companies exist, but their cards are really a variation on a debit card, since the entire charged amount is withdrawn from the account on a set date each month.

Prices include a 20 percent value-added tax, so the price you see is the price you pay. Slovenia is not a bargaining culture, though many shops will give you a discount on a television or couch if you pay cash. For any purchase over a hundred euros, it is worth asking.

chapter **seven**

TRAVEL, HEALTH, & SAFETY

Slovenia offers a pleasant Western European travel experience with a few positive twists. No longer an "undiscovered jewel," neither is it overrun with tourists. Slovenians welcome Western visitors and are happy to help with directions and suggestions.

Slovenians enjoy visiting their own country, so when you visit the main sites, it does not feel like an international airport. It is heartwarming to see a group of pensioners getting out of a rented bus, chattering like schoolchildren as they visit a monastery, hilltop castle, or any of Slovenia's many waterfalls for the umpteenth time.

Travel infrastructure in Slovenia is good, which reflects both a love of order and the country's long history of tourism. For over a hundred years visitors have been flocking to take the cure at the lovely Lake Bled, and even in the nineteenth century well-heeled travelers could get there by train and stay at the many hotels. Similarly, the astounding limestone caves at Postojna and Škocjan have been attracting groups of visitors since at least 1819. Now, as then, these sites remain must-sees.

Slovenia is a dream holiday destination for both children and parents: you never have to drive far,

playgrounds are plentiful, and there is a variety of activities for the little ones (from public swimming pools, to cave tours, to easy hiking trails, to castles aplenty). During the summer months there are numerous outdoor puppet and theater performances for children. Keep your eyes peeled for posters advertising upcoming events, or check out the events listings in the newspaper.

GETTING TO SLOVENIA

The main airport is at Brnik, thirty minutes from Ljubljana. However, Slovenia's conveniently small size and the plethora of neighboring countries means there are other ways of getting here. Zagreb (Croatia), Graz (Austria), and Trieste (Italy) are temptingly close, and each of these cities' airports is just minutes by car from the Slovenian border.

The most convenient international train connections are from Munich, Vienna, and Zagreb. The train from Budapest is direct but slow (take snacks with you, as there is no restaurant car for the eight-hour journey to Ljubljana), and now there is only one direct connection from Venice, aimed at night owls.

PUBLIC TRANSPORTATION

Trains

The quality, frequency, and punctuality of trains in Slovenia depend on when and where you want to travel. Whereas getting from Celje to Maribor is easy, traveling the 160 miles from Ptuj to Nova Gorica takes at least six hours because you have to switch lines so often. Trains are clean and relatively new, with the exception of those used on the branch lines. Delays are no more frequent

than in neighboring Austria. Because of the landscape, trains can seldom go full throttle as they travel alongside the winding rivers carved through the hilly terrain.

Trains on the main line between Maribor and Ljubljana run often, and there are over two dozen trains per day between these cities. Between 5:00 a.m. and early evening the next train will always be leaving within half an hour or so. In other words, you can simply show up and, at worst, kill some time in the station café.

Just showing up is not wise when traveling on the main line from Ljubljana to the coastal town of Koper, as there are only five trains a day. Careful planning is required for traveling to villages and towns on branch lines, where there are often no trains on Sundays. When seeking out a small village, it's easier to travel on a workday.

There are three types of trains, of which the *potniški vlak* (basically, slow train) is the least expensive. These milk trains are ideal for short distances and stop at every hamlet. Intercity (IC) and Eurocity (EC) trains cost slightly more but are faster. You may board one of these trains with a simple ticket for the *potniški vlak*, but you will have to pay an onboard supplement.

Intercity Slovenia (ICS) trains require a (free) seat reservation, which comes with the ticket. A small warning: if you have an international ticket and transfer to an ICS for the Slovenian portion of the journey, you must make a reservation at a

Slovenian station before boarding the train. Slovenians find it pedantic to heed seat reservation numbers, however, and conductors are relaxed about this freedom of movement.

Buses

For traveling to a village that is off the rail lines, buses are the main option. Most buses are clean and reliable, though not glamorous. They tend to be punctual and then some—drivers sometimes go boldly forth a minute or two ahead of schedule if no one is waiting at the roadside stop.

Tickets can be purchased ahead of time at larger town stations or simply from the driver as you board. Keep track of your ticket, because there are inspections. If someone gets on your bus from the middle of nowhere and starts asking you for something, it's not a vagabond but the ticket inspector.

There are a few drawbacks to bus travel in Slovenia. Not many older drivers speak English, so writing down your destination can save minutes of sign language. Because many roadside stations have no schedule posted, check online beforehand (www.ap-ljubljana.si/). Similarly, warn or remind the driver well ahead of time when you plan to get off at one of these small stations. Drivers are usually good at remembering where tourists want to disembark, and simply moving to the front of the bus when you feel you must be near your destination is enough to remind them.

Slovenian bus drivers have a reputation for surliness, and you may encounter this when trying to get basic information from them (though they may be kinder to English-speaking foreigners). The real peril on buses is sonic bombardment from their tinny sound systems: if the driver is over forty, polka music is guaranteed; if the driver is young, expect a pounding beat; if you are very unlucky, you'll find yourself listening to twenty minutes or more of death announcements. Travelers and drivers alike have developed a resistance to background noise. Asking the driver to diminish the din may elicit a quizzical look: what loud radio?

City Transportation

Once upon a time there was a small streetcar network in Ljubljana, and today officials are surely kicking themselves for having torn up the rails in the 1950s. Now local buses are the only option in Ljubljana, and also in Maribor. Only recently did Ljubljana Public Transport come up with a card system that allows passengers to transfer between lines. Before summer 2010, traveling just two stops on two different bus routes required double payment.

Passengers must now purchase an Urbana Card from a kiosk, bus station, or Urbanomat machine, and then load it with credit. You swipe the card when boarding the bus (twice if two are traveling on the same card). The maximum time allowed on

a single fare is ninety minutes, including transfers; this hour and a half easily covers all of the transportation network. Ljubljana Public Transport promises a Tourist Card allowing for twenty-four, forty-eight, or seventy-two hours of travel as well as museum discounts in the near future.

Many bus stops now have digital schedules, but the tiny maps posted on bus shelters remain difficult to decipher. You're better off just asking a friendly local for help. Like their colleagues on interregional buses, city bus drivers are on a tight schedule and will not always be patient. At some stops there will be a line of buses on various routes, meaning you might have to walk back four buses or fifty yards. Expecting your bus to stop again when it reaches the front of the line is a risky strategy.

If the weather's fine, and the Ljubljana city center is your aim, you can do without the bus. During peak hours, both buses and roads are very crowded, and it can sometimes be faster to walk between the main tourist attractions. Much of the center, including the entire old town, is a crisscross of beautiful pedestrian zones that make for great walks but circuitous driving routes.

TAXIS

Fierce competition among companies means it's easy to find a taxi in Ljubljana. Since the city is small and many of the hotels are centrally located, walking from the train station is a comfortable option. As with buses, the combination of pedestrian zones and one-way streets can add extra driving miles to a short distance. What may look like an unnecessary joy ride is usually the only way of getting by car from A to B.

Slovenian taxi drivers are generally honest and quite friendly, but the fares in Ljubljana can be exorbitant, sometimes exceeding ten euros for a mile or so of city travel. A rule of thumb: companies driving (even beat-up) Mercedes are pricier than others. As everywhere, make sure that the meter is running, and don't be shy about demanding a bill or receipt. As we have seen, rounding up rather than actual tipping is the custom.

Outside Ljubljana, taxis are a reasonably inexpensive alternative to public transportation, and they are widely available in any town. In Celje, for example, you can get anywhere within the town limits for the price of a large coffee or a beer. On Sundays and other days when the train schedule's pickings are slim, consider cabbing it to the nearest point of interest. It can also be worthwhile taking a taxi for longer distances when three or more are traveling and willing to split the fare; every cabbie has a story about shuttling a passenger all the way to Vienna, Budapest, or Zagreb. Make sure to arrange the price with the driver beforehand.

DRIVING

The Slovenian road network is well maintained, and many Slovenians prefer driving over public transportation. But be warned: the good-natured Slovenian becomes a menace behind the wheel, especially once outside the city. Only on the roads do the Slovenians appear typically Balkan and Mediterranean in spirit. On local roads, expect aggression, great velocity, and much risk taking, including drivers' firm belief that they can see

around corners and through hills. This combination is as deadly as it is surprising in a mild-mannered people, and the series of flowers and candles one sees on straight stretches of road bear witness to Slovenia's tragically high automobile death rate. Be careful: look and look again at all intersections, regardless of what color light you see, and do not roar off immediately on the green, because you may crash into Evel Knievel racing a red.

Slovenian highways cover the distance between all major towns, and the state is busily working to add more miles. There are plenty of gas stations (the price of gas is the same everywhere, as it is controlled by the state) and all have snack bars or restaurants providing human fuel, too. Massive traffic jams are few and far between. There is one exception to the rule of flow: in summer, every Slovenian, Dutchman, and German heads to the Slovenian or Croatian coast, so highway jams in the southwest of the country are common. A highway toll sticker, or "vignette," which can be purchased at gas stations and border crossings on the way to Slovenia, is required for Slovenian highways. These used to be available only for six months or a full year, but Slovenia has since bowed to European Union pressure (the EU ruled that this half-year minimum was discriminatory to EU citizens just zipping through the country), and travelers can now buy a weekly or a monthly sticker. Controls are strict. There are no police

RULES OF THE ROAD

- European Union citizens do not require a special permit, but drivers from other continents must have an international driver's license.
- Slovenians drive on the right, and the rules of the road are much the same as elsewhere in Europe.
- Traffic lights are placed on the near side of intersections.
- Right turns on red lights are illegal.
- The low beams must always be turned on.
- Each car must have a safety kit, including a warning triangle and a fluorescent vest.
- The blood alcohol limit is 0.05 percent.
- Speed limits are 50 kmph (30 mph) in villages and towns, 90 kmph (55 mph) on regional roads, 100 kmph (62 mph) on highways, and 130 kmph (81 mph) on expressways. Speeding fines are stiff!

scams, however, and officers will not stop you to give you an invented fine. Police officers are less robotic than their Anglophone colleagues and you may well find them humorous . . . or sarcastic.

Curiously, car rental agencies do not let you take certain brands of German cars into Slovenia. Bear this in mind if you were planning to rent a BMW, Audi, or Volkswagen in Munich to drive down to Slovenia.

Radio Slovenia International provides regular traffic reports and updates in English, and you can also call the Automobile Association of Slovenia (Avto-Moto Zveza Slovenije) at (01) 530-5300 for information in English. When the wind is particularly fierce, trailers are banned from stretches of highway between Postojna and the coast. In winter, mountain passes such as the Vršič Pass in the northwest and the Ljubelj Pass (German: Loibl) are often closed. On a culinary note: if traveling from Maribor to Ljubljana, stop for a *krof* at Trojane, the birthplace of this typically Slovenian donut.

CYCLING

Hilly Slovenia is the strong-legged cyclist's dream: splendid scenery, never too far to travel to the next village or campsite, and a network of regional cycling routes. Once again, dangerous drivers ruin the idyll, and cyclists should avoid main roads as much as possible. There are plenty of quieter alternative routes. Be aware that even on marked routes (as opposed to paths, which are reserved for two-wheelers) one often shares space with drivers who are used to owning the road. Stay far to the right as you enjoy the scenery!

OFF THE BEATEN PATH

It's never far to the next attraction in Slovenia, and a tip for tourists is to get off the beaten paths.

By all means, visit the capital of Ljubljana, the beautiful coastal regions, and stop for the obligatory *kremšnita* and *kava* (cream cake and coffee) in Bled, but note that other regions are equally lovely and far less visited. What's more, the locals are refreshingly glad to have visitors, and you may find yourself with a free personal guide for a museum in Ptuj or a small out-of-the-way church in Bela Krajina, or an individual tour through small Karst caves. You may see a telephone number posted near the entrance to a village museum—you can call to summon a key keeper to unlock the doors just for you.

WHERE TO STAY

Slovenia offers a range of accommodation, from hotels to suit all budgets, to hostels and apartments, as well as campsites and tourist farms in the country. In Ljubljana and at the coast, booking ahead is a must in summer. Slovenians' penchant for cleanliness means that hotels are neat, tidy, and well run. Because many smaller hotels do not require a deposit, reconfirming your reservations a few days before you arrive is always wise. Customer service will not always be the well-oiled machine of American hotels, but you can be assured of a decent breakfast and a willingness to help.

Recently, over a dozen hostels have opened up in Ljubljana and, thanks to this, staying there for a few days no longer sinks the budget—there is a shortage of moderately priced hotels in the capital. The ultra-funky Celica hostel led the way in 2003. Housed in a former military prison in the artistic and grungy free-for-all Metalkova area near the Ljubljana train station, each room was decorated by a different artist. The hostel also features a prayer or meditation room, regular art exhibits and concerts, and a movable feast of young and groovy travelers. Most hostels are independent, and thus do not require a Hostelling International membership. There are no age restrictions.

In the countryside, tourist farms are a superb and inexpensive option. Rated with apples rather than stars, these farms come with a variety of perks. A family-run one-apple farm will be closest to a true rural experience, offering little more than a budget place to sleep, while a four-apple farm has many of the amenities of a hotel. These are great places to meet real Slovenians.

KEY DESTINATIONS AND ACTIVITIES

Cities and Towns

Ljubljana. Visit the cathedral, stroll the streets, and have a drink by the Ljubljanica River.
Piran. Head to this coastal town, and imagine you're in a smaller, more peaceful Venice.
Maribor. Party with the Mariborčani during the Lent Festival (late June to early July).
Kamnik. A gorgeous and compact town a stone's throw from the Alps.

Nature

The Logar Valley. Splendid Alpine surroundings ideal for picnics and hiking.
White-water rafting on the Soča River. Or the Kolpa. Or the Savinja. Or the Krka…
Hiking. Find a trail to match your fitness level.
Karst caves. The Postojna and Škocjan caves are the most famous, but in smaller, less-visited ones you can have the stalagmites and stalactites all to yourself.
Castles. Take your pick! In Ptuj, Celje, and Ljubljana, they keep watch over the city;

Predjama Castle emerges from the rocks, and dozens more perch on lonely hilltops.

Culture

Visit a monastery at Žiče, Kostanjevica, Stična, or Olimje (with its adjacent chocolate factory).

The Technical Museum of Slovenia at Bistra pri Vrhniki shows technical development.

Take a wine-tasting tour in one of Slovenia's several wine regions.

Go to a folklore festival and party in Bela Krajina. It may change your life.

HEALTH

Slovenia has a complicated mixture of public and private health services, and private doctors are sometimes covered by public insurance (the difference being that those who pay cash can skip the line). Though Slovenians grumble about the quality of service, it is quite good, and you can confidently head to a town's centralized medical center or hospital, which is where the majority of doctors work. Most doctors, and all younger doctors, will speak English well enough. However, it is very difficult to make sense of most Slovenian hospitals, so find a local to help you navigate the Kafkaesque doors, corridors, and forms.

EU nationals' home insurance suffices for Slovenia, while others should secure insurance before arriving. Recommended vaccinations are as for most European countries (hepatitis A, a flu shot during winter months, and the usual measles-mumps-rubella vaccine; hikers should consider a tick-borne encephalitis vaccine). Larger towns and cities have twenty-four-hour pharmacies. Note that pharmacies have strict control over everything remotely medical, including basics like aspirin and some types of bandages.

If you head for the hills, wear proper boots and take extra clothes because temperatures drop quickly in the mountains. Also, remember to take plenty of water (the tap water in Slovenia is fine).

Ticks are a problem in early spring and summer. Whenever you go hiking, be sure to cover your legs and to inspect yourself carefully in order to avoid Lyme disease.

Brown bears are less common than ticks, but that is small comfort if you happen to encounter one of Slovenia's estimated five hundred. In any case, these bears do not snack on humans. As a tourist Web site explains, "We can say that in their encounter the man and the bear feel pretty much the same"—that is, there is mutual fear.

SAFETY

Slovenian tabloids brazenly claim that Slovenia is the Wild West, with murders aplenty and crimes that would make Billy the Kid blush. This is untrue. Crime rates in Slovenia are lower than elsewhere in Europe and a minimal amount of caution should keep you and your pocketbook safe. Pickpocketing is rare, but be on the lookout for petty theft of knapsacks and laptops. Many of these crimes are linked to drugs, and drug use is surprisingly high for such placid and amiable environs. As anywhere, keep away from large city parks after dark.

Slovenians' greatest fear is not criminality, or bears, or insufficient health insurance, but drafts: they are convinced that currents of air will be the death of them. If you pick up a hitchhiker, she may well ask you to roll up the car window.

chapter **eight**

BUSINESS BRIEFING

The wealthiest of the postcommunist states, Slovenia is often cited as the ideal transition economy. Its per capita GDP places it on the cusp of Western Europe, the workforce is well trained, punctuality is a virtue, there is a keen eye for quality, and the communications and transportation infrastructures are good. Above all, there is the famed Slovenian work ethic, which "even communism failed to destroy."

A glance at a list of Slovenia's largest companies shows a diversified economy, as these companies deal in energy services, pharmaceuticals, financial services, manufacturing, and automobile production. Since 1991, the slow trend has been away from massive, state-controlled companies to small and medium-sized private ones. However, the rush to privatize was nothing like what happened in the former Soviet Union states, and since 2002 privatization has slowed considerably. Taxes are high, and the state still controls the economy to a great degree.

Approximately 66 percent of the workforce are employed in the service industry (with an increasing focus on knowledge-based services such as telecommunications), 32 percent are in industry, and the rest are in agriculture. Along with pharmaceuticals, the major industries include mining (especially lead and zinc) and smelting, as well as manufacturing of automobiles and trucks, and household appliances. The main agricultural areas are potatoes, hops, and sugar beet, along with cattle and poultry. Last, there is a strong corps of tradesmen with medium-sized businesses that build houses, custom-fit windows and doors, make furniture, and so on.

BUSINESS CULTURE

Slovenian business culture is Germanic in its respect for protocol, hierarchy, formality, and division between work time and play time, but more Southern in its relations with employees. One major difference is that Slovenians take their work personally, in the sense that an attack on their performance on a project will be taken as a personal affront. They often seem brutally direct in their barbs and comments, and you may well witness a boss publicly berating a junior colleague.

A few other factors determine the culture of the individual workplace, including the size of the company, whether its head office is in Frankfurt, New York, or Ljubljana, whether it is located in a city or a village, whether it produces financial services or cultural products, and whether the boss is a tradesman or an economist. Large companies with a head office in Ljubljana (as opposed to abroad) are hierarchical, which in plain terms means that the boss wants to sign everything and avoid delegating. Smaller companies are more informal and inclined to use first names, while European multinationals are stricter about processes and protocol. If you are unsure of the way a particular business runs its affairs, err on the side of formality (see page 88 for the difference between *vi* and *ti*), and assume that the boss is the person you want to deal with.

The hiccups in doing business in Slovenia are the same as they would be anywhere else in the Western world, and it is precisely because so much looks the same that the few small differences in the way businesses operate (such as how contracts are handled—see below) may go unnoticed. Things that you may take for granted, such as the need and willingness to work overtime, may not be seen in the same way by your Slovenian partners, and are thus worth pointing out explicitly. For this reason, information flow is the key to harmony and to preventing a business deal from going sour. Be very specific in your instructions and directions.

Slovenians are very aware of condescension, so it is crucial not only to listen to their ideas but to let them know that you are listening and to show appreciation for their input. Your understated nods indicating tacit agreement might go unnoticed: be sure to let your partners, in any busy situation, know that they are involved in the decision making process. After all, they know their business landscape better than you do.

THE CUSTOMER IS NOT ALWAYS THE BOSS

At some level, all Slovenian businesspeople are aware that "the customer is king," but this is not always evident. Treatment in shops and banks can range from coolly distant, through remarkably informal, to downright rude, by American standards. Some of the little things you're used to are missing: employees do not always answer the phone by mentioning the name of the company, post office clerks rarely say, "I'll be with you in a second" as they shuffle their papers right in front of you, and cashiers are not trained to put the cash in your hand, so many a coin goes rolling. Don't be discouraged if a cashier or train station clerk barks at you for some minor transgression such as stacking your basket in the wrong pile or trying to secure both information and a train ticket.

For those brought up on empty service phrases and hollow apologies, this ruggedness is refreshing. It is also a time-saver. If the answer to your question is "no," Slovenian salespeople will not say, "I'm sorry, but at this time we are unable to…" That "no" saves time and words.

Slovenians go for the direct approach, rather than the soft sell. Salespeople don't ease into a sale by talking about the weather for a few minutes, and they are unlikely to push the most expensive product on you. The downside to this sales approach is that they may be slow to suggest an alternative, and a conversation may go like this: "Do you have Acme brand detergent?" "No." They may have seven other types of detergent, but that is not what you asked for!

Many Slovenians and foreigners are quick to blame this apathy on the legacy of socialism. In the past, sellers sometimes had a monopoly on goods and there was simply nowhere else to go. In the view of the antisocialists, employees, used to perks like having meals and commuting costs covered by the employer and the guarantee of a job for life, became complacent and acquired a sense of entitlement. This, however, is an oversimplification. Modern Slovenian corporate culture is just as much to blame. On the whole, small, independent shops, where the owner is directly involved in the sales process, offer better service. In larger shops and department stores, once you are in the right place, you will find well-informed salespeople to help you.

WOMEN IN BUSINESS

Despite a clear strain of Central European chauvinism, today there is little difference between how men and women are treated in business. Foreign businesswomen are not looked down upon, and they are treated in much the same way as in neighboring Austria.

Whether there is a glass ceiling is debatable. There are a number of prominent female businesswomen, and about a third of all managers and senior officials are female. On the other hand, most women in business occupy the middle rather than the upper echelons of the corporate structure. Wage equality is also a weak point, as on average men earn almost one-third more than women.

MEETINGS

A rule of thumb when setting up a meeting is to go as high up the ladder as possible. If a secretary or underling appears uncooperative, be persistent, as there is a Slovenian habit of rejecting the out-of-the-ordinary, even if it's something as simple as a new business proposal. In midsized companies this means you should arrange things with the boss. When planning a meeting from outside the country, set up direct e-mail or telephone contact with the boss; if this is not possible, try to deal consistently with the same individual at the company. Especially when meetings are arranged over the phone, and when you are on a tight schedule, confirm and reconfirm in writing.

Slovenians love their meetings, and if a few parties are involved in the business deal, be sure to arrange for all to be in the boardroom. Once in the actual meeting room, you can expect the meeting to be fairly straightforward: some cursory introductions, an offer of coffee, and then down to business (the smaller the company, the longer the conversational warm-up). Usually the boss will conduct the meeting. There will be an agenda of sorts, but Slovenians tend to regard agendas as guidelines, and may meander around considerably.

You will notice far more repetition than you are used to in English-style meetings. Do not expect understatement and brevity. In line with this, you may want to add an extra line or two or summation or emphasis to ensure that *your* point has been made and understood.

Note that business lunches are not usual, and if they occur at all they are more likely to follow the meeting and be rather informal. There is a profound irony here, because many deals are hammered out or refined not in the boardroom but in the café. This is because the division between business and pleasure is fluid, and the apparent autocrat who dominated the meeting will probably come down to earth once the formidable expectations of Slovenian meeting culture are put aside. Get personal!

PRESENTATIONS

Slovenian presentations can be formal to the point of stiffness. Be aware of this when presenting your project at a meeting. Visual aids are welcome, especially because you will probably be presenting in English, and Slovenians' English often sounds better than it is (since many have adopted American-sounding accents from television). Humor, however, can backfire in presentations because, even if understood and shared, it can harm your credibility. In Slovenian business culture, joking and working are two separate domains.

If you do opt for levity, be sure to tell the audience exactly what point the anecdote or joke is there to illustrate, and how it is linked to your goal. "I mention that because . . . " or "All kidding aside, here we see . . . " are useful phrases. On a positive note, Slovenians are attuned to differing presentation cultures and may be more willing to laugh in English.

NEGOTIATIONS

In terms of negotiations, Slovenians are more relaxed than Americans, but far less relaxed (as well as far less macho) than their Balkan neighbors. If it is possible to give lip service to *not* being consensual, many Slovenian businesspeople

do exactly that. In other words, they may say, with Germanic firmness, that they will not move on the price—only to do so, eventually. They appreciate straightforward approaches, and you are unlikely to ruin a deal by flouting protocol or addressing somebody by his first name.

Because of the hierarchical nature of Slovenian business culture, you will be negotiating with one or two individuals rather than a team. If you are not talking directly with the boss, the chances are that your counterpart will have to ask the boss to sign on the dotted line before the deal is done.

Large Slovenian companies get back to you quickly, but some smaller companies are rather lax in the little things than make a deal go smoothly. The attitude there seems to be that if the business is installing windows or printing promotional material, why be concerned with a smooth paper trail and neat receipts?

CONTRACTS

In Slovenia, a lot of small business deals are done on a handshake and a mountain of trust, so establishing trustworthiness is crucial. Though the law regulates contractual agreements, Slovenians maintain a relaxed attitude toward them—they may expect you to start work before the contract is sealed, and in exceptional cases they may expect freelancers to sign a contract only *after* the job has been completed (a practice that is, in fact, illegal). On the other hand, individuals may send goods before they get your cash on the casual and confident assumption that you'll pay sooner or later. If you have provided a service, *later* is when you can expect to see your money. It may be worth (gently) reminding your client that you will not commence work until the contract is signed.

The business law is continental and is based on interpretation and the letter of the law rather than precedence. It is a wise idea to have a Slovenian lawyer peruse the contract before you sign it.

MANAGING DISPUTES

In the Workplace

For all their bluntness, Slovenians go to great lengths to avoid disputes and open conflict in the workplace. They take any comments and questions about their performance personally. If a dispute arises, it is usually because of money, as Slovenians are willing to tolerate poor working conditions and minor harassment as long as the hands are kept off the pocketbook. Whereas workers in other countries might speak up immediately when something irks them, Slovenians quietly grumble to themselves until they reach a breaking point.

As we have seen, small problems may not be addressed until it's too late. You should confirm and reconfirm that all is well with your business partner or counterpart (even if it means asking person X how person Y is feeling).

Especially when criticism comes from outsiders, Slovenian skin is paper-thin. This means that they may interpret your innocent little questions as a heinous personal attack. A possible way around this problem might be to refer to a department or work sector rather than an individual, but this strategy has its weaknesses. Because Slovenians love to hide within a collective (because they hate to stand out), your target audience might not realize that you are addressing him or her.

Offering praise as a prelude to criticism is not generally part of Slovenian culture, since Slovenians take the good for granted and thus not worthy of special mention. Outsiders, though, might want to note the positive before moving on to the less-than-stellar. Genuine concerns and criticism should be discussed privately rather than in a full boardroom.

Business Disputes

Many of those with grievances choose an indirect path when seeking remedy; they will speak to someone, who will speak to someone else. This mysterious telephone game is surprisingly effective. When speaking with someone about a difficulty, be prepared to read between the lines. On the other hand, a colleague might go straight to the boss to inform him or her of a little something you've done wrong, rather than speaking directly to you. They do not like face-to-face confrontation.

If a dispute is taken to court, be aware that the process is lengthy and complicated, even if fair. By Slovenian law, whoever loses the case is required to cover the legal expenses of the other party.

chapter **nine**

COMMUNICATING

LANGUAGE

Language is the cornerstone of Slovenian national identity, and accordingly there are strict laws limiting the use of foreign languages. There is very little chauvinism or overt linguistic nationalism in Slovenia. Slovenians appreciate that their language is spoken by a relatively small number of people. They are well versed in other languages, with English being the clear leader among young people.

Contemporary Standard Slovenian is the language taught in schools. This is what Slovenians will try to speak in order to sound "educated," and it is also what politicians strive for if they don't want to be pegged to a particular region. Contemporary Standard Slovenian is, like "the Queen's English," invented in the sense that it does not precisely match any spoken dialect. It is closest to the dialects spoken in the geographical center of Slovenia.

A Slavic language, Slovenian belongs to the same extended family as Russian, Polish, and Czech. Its closest relatives are Serbian/Bosnian/ Croatian, Macedonian, and Bulgarian, and if you

Misli širše
Obisk avstrijskega kanclerja Wernerja Faymanna
Premier Pahor
v bran slovenski
Po besedah slovenskega premiera uveljavitev 7. člena
Avstrije, temveč njena mednarodna obveza – Fayman
BRDO PRI KRANJU – V Sloveniji se je včeraj na delovnem obisku mudil avstrij
ložnosti se je sestal s slovenskim premierom Borutom Pahorjem. Sogovorn
sti namenila zglednemu gospodarskemu sodelovanju med državama in po
veda se nista mogla izogniti položaju slovenske manjšine na
njevanja sedmega člena avstrijske državne
dobrih odnosih med
šiti na sodišču

speak Slovenian you will understand a fair amount of those languages. And yet, Slovenian clearly stands on its own (for example, "late" in Slovenian means "pregnant" in Croatian).

There are between forty and fifty subdialects and seven or eight major dialect groups. Slovenians often explain that if each sticks to his dialect a person from the Hungarian border will have great difficulty understanding a person from the Adriatic coast. Television interviews in Slovenian with individuals from the region of Prekmurje are sometimes subtitled when the speaker's dialect is deemed impenetrable for the rest of the country's listeners.

Many Slovenians proudly proclaim that their grammar—with its six grammatical cases (nominative, genitive, dative, accusative, locative, and instrumental) and its curious dual form—is among the most difficult in the world. This means that only a linguistic genius will be able to master it without formal instruction.

The Dual Form

Slovenians are very proud of the dual grammatical form. Whereas most languages are content with a singular and a plural, Slovenian has a way of saying "the two of us," "the two of you," "the two of them," and so on. The expression "*midve sva šli*" translates as "we went," but in fact it transmits the information: "the two of us (both female) went." "*Midva sva šla*" is either "the two of us (both male) went" or "the two of us (one female and one male) went." Learn a phrase or two in the dual, and you're sure to impress the locals.

Learning Slovenian

For all the claims about how difficult Slovenian is, there is some good news for learners. Slovenian uses a Latin alphabet rather than a Cyrillic one, and most letters are pronounced more or less in the same as in English. A further blessing is that words are written phonetically: the *feniks* rises from the ashes, celibacy is *celibat*, and a Celt is a *kelt*.

However, there aren't many vowels in Slovenian words, and words such as *trg*, *prt*, *smrt* (the words for market square, tablecloth, death) to an outsider look as if they're missing something. English speakers could argue that there is in fact a short, albeit unwritten, vowel sound in the above words, as *prt* and *smrt* more or less rhyme with "Bert."

In addition to relatively standard pronunciation, there is another plus for learners. Whereas a mere decade ago the lack of and poor quality of language textbooks could lead one to despair, things have recently improved. Today there are plenty of resources awaiting eager learners—from textbooks to formal grammars, CD packages, and DVDs, not to mention about two million Slovenians eager to help out if asked.

While no nation discourages others from learning its language, Slovenians are simply joyous when visitors make the effort. However, as you marble-mouth Slovenian, be aware that they are not used to hearing their language spoken with a Western foreign accent, so don't be put off by puzzled looks as they try to figure out what you've just tried to say (in more tourist-oriented centers, they'll just switch to English). One strange note is that Slovenians are slow to correct grammatical errors. You will be praised for every two-word phrase uttered or cup of *kava* ordered, but your mistakes may pass without comment.

Pronunciation

There are a few curiosities in the twenty-five-letter Slovenian alphabet. Some letters (q, w, x, and y) are missing and three others have been added.

The letter "q" exists only in imported words. Otherwise, it is efficiently replaced by "*kv*" in Slovenian, thus *slovenska kvaliteta* for *Slovenian quality*. "X" has a similar phonetic replacement (“*ks*”), so that *xenon* is spelled *ksenon*. Slovenian does not have the letter “w,” which has been categorically replaced by the v-sound—Belgian waffles are *belgijski vaflji*. This leads us to “*j*,” which in Slovenian is pronounced the same as an English “y,” and which is written where English pronounces the “y” sound but does not write it—we write “dahlia,” for example, but say “dah-lee-ya.” Slovenians write *dalija*.

In Slovenian three consonants—*č*, *š*, and *ž*—have what is called a “superscript diacritic,” and what can more charmingly and helpfully be called a “little roof” (a literal translation of *strešica*). English speakers have a habit of simply ignoring them; but they do affect pronunciation and are not merely cosmetic marks.

Č sounds like English “ch” as in “child”; *š* is like the “sh” in “shin”; and *ž* is like the “s” in “treasure.” Only two consonant sounds are pronounced altogether differently. The Slovenian “*c*” is pronounced like the sound repeated in “tsetse fly” or at the end of “Ritz.” Less important, because it does not drastically affect meaning, is the sound quality of the Slovenian “*r*,” which is rolled. This is formed with the tip of the tongue rather than emerging from further back, as in American English. Try saying *riba, raca, rak* (fish, duck, crab) through a straw or biting on a fingertip and you’ll be halfway there. Ask a Slovenian to help you improve, and see if he can keep a straight face while doing so.

Though most Slovenians will get your point when you mispronounce one letter in a word, keep in mind that confusion grows exponentially. If you want to buy a train ticket to the village of "Šmarje," the ticket seller will probably understand "Shmar-juh," but not necessarily "smar-juh." If in doubt, write it down!

PRACTICE THE BASICS

The differences in pronunciation between English and Slovenian are few, and you can master the basics in less than an hour. Practice with words and names taken from other languages:

bowling *bovling*
cello *čelo*
hockey *hokej*
pizzeria *picerija*
Quaker *kveker*
sandwich *sendvič*
Shostakovich Šostakovič
sexy sextet *seksi sekstet*
Tchaikovsky Čajkovski
tweed *tvid*
weekend *vikend* (usually "cottage" in Slovenian)
xenophobia *ksenofobija*
xylophone *ksilofon*

Wordiness

The history of wordiness in Slovenia is long and proud, and has been fueled by both the *über*-bureaucratic Habsburg and communist traditions. Slovenians themselves laugh at opaque, clause-rich sentences that seem to go nowhere, but the habit continues.

When it comes to formal writing and speaking, Slovenians are greatly impressed by details, facts, numbers, and lists. A reader will often be halfway through an information-rich newspaper or magazine piece before receiving any inkling of what the journalist's opinion or point is. Columnists aren't avoiding the issue, they're just moving at the more leisurely Slovenian prose pace, while establishing intellectual credibility by showing how much they know.

BODY LANGUAGE

There are no typically Slovenian gestures, which means that you will not inadvertently offend someone with a wave of the hand.

Slovenians display little public emotion, and this is reflected in their body language and demeanor: they don't screech and holler, they don't stand too close to each other, and they don't gesticulate much. However, this physical aspect of conversation changes as one nears the coast and predictably, more Italianate gestures, less personal space, and more hugging become evident.

A FEW PHRASES

Dobro jutro Good morning (used until 9:00 a.m.)

Dober dan Hello (literally, "Good day")

Dober večer Good evening

Lahko noč Good night

Nazvidenje Good-bye

Adijo 'Bye (informal)

Kako ste? Kako si? How are you? (formal/informal. Expect a sincere answer.)

Ja Yes

Ne No

Oprostite! Oprosti! Excuse me! (formal/informal)

Prosim Please

Hvala Thank you

Dober tek! Enjoy your meal, or *Bon appétit!*

Na zdravje! Cheers! (literally, "To health!")

Ali govorite angleško? Do you speak English?

In ex-Yugoslavia Slovenians had the reputation of being cold and reserved in comparison to their Balkan neighbors. If you base your assumptions solely on fleeting contact with cashiers, ticket takers, and the like, you may find them apathetic, glum, or borderline rude. This can be boiled down to three cultural differences. First, older Slovenians are unlikely to smile just because they are selling you a beer or stamping your train ticket. They don't apologize if their jacket happens to whisk against yours on the bus. And outside tourist areas visitors (especially nonwhites) can expect stares from curious and harmless older people.

THE MEDIA

For a small population, Slovenia has an impressive array of newspapers, magazines, television channels, and radio stations. Look at any kiosk's well-stocked shelves to confirm the presence of a thriving, healthy press.

Among the main daily news sources there is little overt political bias. Competition is fierce as companies fight for their slice of this small market pie. Also, because so many Slovenians are multilingual and because so many live within range of foreign television and radio signals, Slovenian media outlets fight both domestic and international competition. In terms of actual ownership, however, only commercial television is controlled to any degree by foreign investors.

English-language news and entertainment is everywhere in Slovenia. Foreign movies and television programs are subtitled rather than dubbed, and kiosks in towns and cities stock a range of English-language news sources. Public libraries will have plenty of English magazines for your perusal.

Newspapers

The main and most trusted news sources continue to be traditional print newspapers or their online equivalents. The three largest Slovenian broadsheets are *Delo*, *Dnevnik*, and *Večer*, each of which is centrist or slightly left-of-center. *Delo* strives to be national in focus, while the latter two are more concerned with Ljubljana and Maribor respectively (the smaller *Primorske novice* serves the region near the Italian border). The tabloid *Slovenske novice* offers bold headlines and titillating and sensationalist stories, along with pictures of scantily clad celebrities or other models. Though the state has much financial stake in each of these newspapers, there is no obvious or direct government censorship, and partisanship is not a problem. To take *Delo* as an example, while some rightists claim that it is overly leftist and reflects the paper's communist past, leftists complain that it has swung too far to the right. The truth and the editorial stance are somewhere in the middle.

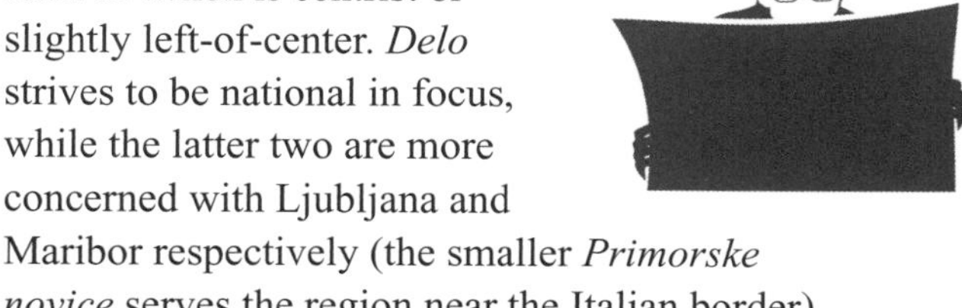

The monthly *Slovenia Times* is the sole English-language newspaper. Written primarily by Slovenians rather than expats, the *Slovenia Times* offers you the news of the land as seen through Slovenian eyes. This is especially helpful for those looking to do business here.

Television

The excellent public television RTV Slovenia is financed primarily by mandatory television licenses. In other words, each household pays a monthly bill (which is not the same as the cable bill). RTV is required by law to provide programming to suit the needs of a wide spectrum of the Slovenian population, including Slovenians living just beyond the country's borders and the official Italian and Hungarian minorities in Slovenia. Their mandate is to provide news, cultural education, sports, and higher-brow entertainment to all Slovenians, and they fulfill this mandate admirably. Any given week will yield fascinating interviews with prominent Slovenians and non-Slovenians alike, domestic and foreign documentaries, and a handful of quality foreign movies.

The other major players in the television market are Pop TV and Kanal A, both owned by

an American company. They are populist in scope and, accordingly, these channels broadcast plenty of good and bad Hollywood movies and comedy series (all subtitled).

With the rise of Internet programming and the quantity of foreign cable channels available, the Slovenian television landscape is changing quickly. And yet Slovenians continue to take their old-fashioned public television seriously: when the government recently proposed amendments to RTV's legal status, citizens sensed privatization urges and overwhelmingly rejected the idea in a referendum.

Radio

As with television, the law dictates that RTV Slovenia must cover the entire nation and its perceived interests. There are three main stations (conveniently known as 1, 2, and 3) focusing on information, lighter entertainment and mainstream music, and culture. In addition to this, Radio Slovenia International broadcasts much of its programming in English. Another Slovenia-wide station is Radio Ognjišče, owned by the Slovenian Catholic Church and catering to the wishes of its faithful. Most radio stations are local and have a small catchment area. Dial spinners will be struck by two things: the abundance of stations addressing a tiny local audience, and the apparent sameness of entertainment content. Those in search of polka will always find a tune or two, while those in search of 1970s and 1980s pop will find three or four stations pumping out vintage Michael Jackson and ABBA.

INTERNET AND E-MAIL

More Slovenians have broadband Internet than any other Europeans, and a sure way of insulting them is to doubt Internet availability. As a traveler, you'll always be able to go online somewhere. Wireless service in the larger hotels and, increasingly, in trendier cafés, is a given.

Unless you are in a shack in the hills or living very far from any urban center, there are generally at least two or three service providers offering increasingly attractive packages (starting at just over ten euros per month for a basic service). Often they'll throw in digital TV and telephone services for just a few euros more. In the past, consumers had to wait several weeks to be hooked up, but this is no longer the case. The only downside to these deals is that the standard contract is two years.

TELEPHONES

In a recent survey, Ljubljana was found to be the best city in the world to lose your cellular phone. Why? Because *Ljubljančani* are most likely to turn in a lost phone. This is as much an indication of honesty as a reflection of the fact that every Slovenian already seems to own several cell phones. Competition between providers means that new deals are offered on a regular basis, and Slovenians regularly upgrade to the latest and greatest model. Before purchasing a cell phone, it's worthwhile asking around to see if someone has an old one for donation or rental. Calls within the European Union have recently dropped in price as companies no longer overcharge clients for calling Austria or Italy. However, wily phone companies recoup this lost potential revenue in calls from Slovenia to Croatia and other nearby non-EU countries (on this note, be very careful in border regions—you may pay through the nose if your phone's roaming function connects you to a Croatian network when you're still in Slovenian territory). Using international services is generally more expensive, and you might want to acquire a Slovenian SIM card for the duration of your visit. For short-term stays, prepaid calling cards from a Slovenian operator are an inexpensive option.

For a nation that is not notably chatty, Slovenia has a lively cell phone culture, and people will blithely interrupt a conversation or business meeting to pick up a ringing phone. Don't take it personally. On any bus or train there will be half a dozen zesty calls in progress, and Slovenians duly yank out their telephones whenever they have a minute to spare or kill.

Traditional phone booths of the Superman variety are disappearing fast. Pay phones require a phone card, meaning that calling is a two-step process: only after buying a card from a kiosk or *trafika* (tobacconist) can you make your call. Very few of these soon-to-be relics accept credit cards.

The weak link in the Slovenian phone system is Telekom Slovenia's ineffective online telephone directory. Though it is better than it used to be, the search options remain poor in Slovenian and worse in English. Anything other than a simple search requires a complicated registration process. For locating businesses, a regular Internet search is always preferable; to find someone's home or private cell number, first find a fluent speaker of Slovenian to help you. Better yet, locate an old-fashioned telephone book at the hotel reception desk.

MAIL

The Slovenian postal service is remarkably efficient, and letters sent by regular mail to a Slovenian destination arrive the very next day. Airmailing packages internationally is not only relatively inexpensive; it comes with a free tracking service that lets you follow your package from Maribor to Manhattan. If you are mailing goods overseas, ask the teller to help you find the cheapest solution—sometimes squashing a book and a T-shirt into a padded envelope can save you a box and a bundle of cash.

There are no machines dispensing Slovenia's range of pretty stamps, so you have to line up to post your letter (always an adventure in Slovenia). This waiting is made worse by the plethora of services post offices provide: you may spend ten minutes in a two-person line as the individual in front of you performs extravagant banking maneuvers, purchases lottery tickets, sends a telegram and accompanying cuddly toy to a newborn, and—a given in village post offices—chats with the teller. You can buy simple stamps for postcards from a *trafika*, but be sure not to go over (or under!) the strict size and weight limits stipulated by Pošta Slovenije.

CONCLUSION

Slovenians retain an understated and understandable pride in their country, which is why they are delighted to show it off to visitors. Modest through and through, they will not smother you with false affection and overhasty offers of friendship, but if you ask them for help, they will be there for you; otherwise, they will leave you in peace.

The new state inhabits the comfortable space between Germanic rigidness/efficiency and Southern laxness/casualness, but even within that space there is a cultural variety that could be the envy of many larger states. Why so many visitors limit themselves to the Ljubljana-Piran-Bled triangle is a mystery in a place where the next natural or cultural discovery is never far away.

There are very few downsides to Slovenia. Rules and bureaucracy may seem overwhelming at times, but there are usually no dire consequences when something is not in order. This is a minor and necessary irritation—necessary because otherwise one might overlook the orderly manner in which so much of Slovenian society runs. Even with the mountains of paperwork, life will continue, and as long as Slovenians continue to work and tend their gardens it will continue pleasantly, without phoniness and insincerity. If they can avoid sticking out and find some time to celebrate, then all is well.

Further Reading

Cankar, Ivan. *Martin Kačur: The Biography of an Idealist*. Trans. John K. Cox. Budapest: Central European University Press, 2009.

Corsellis, John and Marcus Ferrar. *Slovenia 1945: Memories of Death and Survival after World War II*. London: I. B. Tauris, 2010.

Debeljak, Aleš. *Twilight of the Idols: Recollections of a Lost Yugoslavia*. Fredonia, New York: White Pine Press, 1994.

Granda, Stane. *Slovenia: An Historical Overview*. Ljubljana: Government Communication Office, 2008.

Jančar, Drago et al. *The Day Tito Died: Contemporary Slovenian Short Stories*. London, Boston: Forest Books, 1993.

Johnson Debeljak, Erica. *Forbidden Bread*. Berkeley: North Atlantic Books, 2009.

Pahor, Boris. *Necropolis*. Trans. Michael Biggins. Champaign, Il.: Dalkey Archive Press, 2010.

Some Useful Web Sites

www.slovenia.info/
The Slovenia Tourist Board's searchable travel guide.

www.carniola.org/
A New Yorker and Slovenian by choice reflects on cultural differences. Splendidly written.

www.sloveniatimes.com/
The online version of the English language newspaper.

www.avsenik.com/
A pre-taste of Slovenian-style polka.

www.stat.si/eng/index.asp
The Statistical Office of the Republic of Slovenia's fascinating Web site.

www.sta.si/en/
The Slovenian Press Agency. The most up-to-date source for Slovenian news (not free).

Index

Abraham, the 76–77
accommodation 130–32
airports 119
Albanians 19
alcohol 76, 95, 96, 115–16
All Saints' Day *see* Day of Commemoration of the Dead
apartments 97–98, 130
architecture 109
Argentina 20, 35
art 109
Assumption Day 61
Austria 10, 13, 18, 32, 34, 37, 45
authority, attitudes toward 51

banking 116–17
bears, brown 135
Belgrade 32, 36, 49
birthrates 74
body language 154–56
Bosnia and Herzegovina 36
Bosnians 54, 59
Bossman, Peter 54
bureaucracy 50–51, 164
buses 122–24
business culture 137–39
business disputes 146–47
butarice 65

Cankar, Ivan 110
Carantania, Duchy of 22–23
Carnival (Pust) 63–64
castles 132–33
Catholic Church 25, 46, 47
Celje 21, 26, 31, 110, 120
Celje, Counts of 25–26
Celts 21
character 8–9, 44, 51–52, 55–56, 163
Christianity 24
Christmas 60–63
climate 10, 16–17
coffee 86
Cold War 36, 49
communism 36, 44, 49
Communist Party of Slovenia 33
Constitution 18
contracts 144–45
conversation 81–83
corporate culture 140
corruption 42
credit cards 117
crime 135
Croatia 10, 13, 24, 36, 43, 47, 161
Croatians 18
cultural activities 109–12
currency 10, 38, 44
customer not always the boss 139–40
cycling 106, 107, 129

daily routine 100–101
dating 89–91
Day of Commemoration of the Dead (All Saints' Day) 61, 67–68
Day of Independence and Unity 61, 73–74
Day of Uprising Against Occupation 61, 71–72
debit cards 117
Democratic Opposition of Slovenia (DEMOS coalition) 36–37
desserts 113–14
dispute management 145–47
driving 126–29

e-mail 160
Easter 61, 64–66
Easter eggs 66
eating out 114–16
economic transformation 42–43
education 50, 56–57, 93–97
employment 102–3
ethnic makeup 10, 18–20
European Union (EU) 12, 38, 43, 44, 127, 128, 161
Eurozone 23
eye contact 88

family life 92–93
fireworks 65, 66–67
First World War 31–32
folklore festivals 133
food 69, 75–76, 101, 112–14
foreigners, attitude toward 53
France 43
Frankolovo massacre 34
Franks 24
Freisling Manuscripts 24
funerals 77

gardens 100, 164
GDP 136
geography 12–15
German-speaking population 19
Germany 33, 37, 43, 97
gifts 62–63, 68, 75, 87
government 10, 38–40
grape harvesting (*trgatev*) 69
greetings 88
Gypsies *see* Roma

Habsburg Empire 32
Habsburgs 8, 15, 20, 25, 26, 27, 29, 50
handshakes 67, 88, 144
health 50, 133–35
hiking/trekking 107–8, 132, 134
history 20–38
  before Slovenians 20–22
  Slavs and Slovenians 22–23

the Middle Ages 24–27
Reformation and Counter-Reformation 27
Napoleon 27–28
linguistic awakening 28–31
the First World War and a Slavic kingdom 31–33
the Second World War and its aftermath 33–35
communist times 35–36
postcommunist times 36–38
Hitler, Adolf 45
holidays 60–68
public 61, 70–74
hospitals 134
hostels 130, 131
hotels 130, 131
houses 97, 99
housework 93
humor 83–84, 143
Hungarians 10, 18
Hungary 8, 10, 13, 18, 33, 113
Huns 22

Illyrian tribes 21
independence (1991) 8, 20, 37, 44, 47, 70, 73–74
International Women's Day 68
Internet 160
domain 11
programming 159
invitations 86–87
Italians 10, 18
Italy 10, 13, 18, 32, 33, 35, 43, 45

Jančar, Drago 110
Jewish community 48–49

Kamnik 132
Karst region 8, 12, 14, 22
key destinations and activities 132–33
Kingdom of Serbs, Croats, and Slovenians 32
kissing 88
koline 69
Koper 16, 96
Kopitar, Jernej 29
Krpan, Martin 26
Kučan, Milan 37
kurent (mythological beast) 63–64

Lake Bled 118
Lake Cerknica 12
Langobards 22
language 8, 10, 27–31, 37, 45–46, 110, 148–54
the dual 150
a few phrases 155
learning Slovenian 150–51
practice the basics 153
pronunciation 151–53
wordiness 154
Liberation Front 33, 71–72
Ljubljiana 10, 17, 19–20, 21, 27, 28, 30, 48, 73, 96–97, 99, 111, 121, 123, 124–25, 130, 131, 132, 138
Logar Valley 132
Luther, Martin 73

Macedonia 36
Macedonians 59
magazines 156
mail 162–63
making friends 78–91
conversation 81–83
dating 89–91
friends for life 79–80
humor 83–84
invitations 86–87
manners 88
meeting people 80–81
taboo topics 84–85
manners 88
Maribor 10, 13, 17, 19, 48, 69, 96, 99, 111, 120, 121, 132
markets 62, 65, 101
May Day Holiday 61, 72
media 11, 156–60
meetings 141–42
Milošević, Slobodan 36
mineral waters 116
monasteries 133
Montenegro 36
Mount Triglav 14, 17
Murska Sobota 13, 17
music 111–12
Muslims 48
Mussolini, Benito 45

names 74–75
Napoleon Bonaparte 27–28
national holidays 70–74
nationalism 30
NATO 38
Nazis 33, 34
negotations 143–44
New Year 61, 66–67
newspapers 11, 156, 157
Non-Aligned Movement 36
Noricum 21
nouveaux riches 58
Nova Gorica 96, 110, 120

off the beaten path 129–30
office parties 87
Ostrogoths 22
Otto I, Holy Roman Emperor 22
Ottokar II, King of Bohemia 25

Pahor, Boris 110
Pannonian plain 12, 14
Partisans 33, 34, 35
pensions 50
Peterle, Lojze 37
pharmacies 134
pickpocketing 135
Piran 13, 132
Plečnik, Jože 109
Pohorje Mountains 12
police 127–28

politics 40–42
population 10, 18
Postojna limestone caves 118, 132
presentations 143
Prešeren Day 61, 70–71
Prešeren, France 28, 29, 70–71
press 11
prices 117
Prince's Stone 23
privatization 136–37
Protestants 48
Ptuj 21, 63, 120
public holidays 61

queuing 89

radio 11, 156, 159–60
Reformation Day 61, 73
religion 10, 46–49
restaurants 114
rivers 15
Roma (Gypsies) 19, 46–48, 55
Roman Catholicism, Roman Catholics 10, 73
Romans 21–22
Rudolf of Habsburg 25

safety 135
St. Martin's Day 69
Šalamun, Tomaž 110
sales approach 140
Samo, King 22
schools 93–95
Second World War 33–35, 72, 84
self-image 51–52
Serbia 36
Serbian Orthodox Christians 48
Serbians 19, 54
Sestre (Sisters) 53–54
sexual orientation 53–54
shopping 101–2
skiing 106, 108–9
Škocjan limestone caves 118, 132
slippers 103
Slovakia 45
Slovenian Littoral 14
Slovenian People's Party 30
soccer 106
speed limits 128
sports 105–9
Stalin, Joseph 35
State of Slovenians, Croats and Serbs 32
Statehood Day 61, 73, 74
status 57–59
streetcars 123
supermarkets 101
swearing 85

taboo topics 84–85
taxis 125–26
Technical Museum of Slovenia, Bistra pri Vrhniki 133
telephones 11, 160–62
television 11, 149, 156, 158–59
Ten-Day War (1991) 37
territorial smallness 44–45
theater 110–11
ticks 134
tipping 115
Tito, Marshal 33, 35, 36, 48, 49, 84
tolerance 53–55
tourist farms 131–32
trains 120–22
Trieste 35
Trubar, Primož 73
  Abecedarium 27
  Catechism 27
trust 144–45
Turks 26

Ulrich II 26
universities 96–97

vacations 104–5
Valentine's Day 68
Vatican, the 37, 47
Venetian Republic 8

water, drinking 134
weddings 75–76
white-water rafting 132
wine-tasting 133
women in business 141
work ethic 59, 136
working hours 59
writers 110

Yugoslavia 32–37, 42, 43, 45, 71, 84
Yugoslavian Army 37

Zagreb 32
Zedinjena Slovenija 30

Acknowledgments

Thanks to all those who helped me out, including Alenka, Liz Blake, Lisa Botshon, Cecilia Fink, Michelle Gadpaille, Dennis Gurnick, Olaf Hahn, Rick Hughes, Olga and Igor Kabalin, Amy Anne Kennedy and Matic Ačko (photos), Marco Kranjc, Tomaž Laznik, Uroš Mozetič, Barbara Por Hrovat, Donald Reindl, Anthony Rezek, John and Elaine Robinson, Tina and Luka Stok (photos), Andrej Stopar, Barbara Žuran, my students, and the Celje hockey team.